three small

suspects

A Memoir.

Nicholas Horgan

ILLUSTRATIONS
Amanda Gould

COVER & DESIGN
Melanie Maher

PHOTOGRAPHY

Dave Batty

John R Sharp

Published in Australia by Sid Harta Publishers Pty Ltd,
ACN: 007 030 051
23 Stirling Crescent, Glen Waverley, Victoria 3150 Australia
Telephone: +61 3 9560 9920, Facsimile: +61 3 9545 1742
E-mail: author@sidharta.com.au
First published in Australia 2009
This edition published 2009

Horgan, Nicholas James
Three Small Suspects
ISBN: 1-921642-07-6
EAN13: 978-1-921642-07-4

We have great pleasure in contributing a foreword to Nick Horgan's entertaining book.

Our recollections of a young Nick and his family now go back many years. Our bakery was in Poole Street, Motueka and the Horgan's large house was "just over the road". It is now obvious in reading of Nick and his siblings' escapades that we knew very little about them. We did know that they were boisterous but always respectful and polite to us.

Nick's mum and dad were very highly respected in our little community to which they contributed so much. For years Mr Horgan was on the gate for rugby matches at Rugby Park. A real identity. We remember Mrs Horgan mostly for the beautiful gladioli which she grew and her incredible skill with flower arrangements, a talent that her daughter, Veronica, has inherited.

In later years, Nick was a valued employee in our expanding food group. He certainly has drive and lots of initiative.

We wish Nick every succcess with his entertaining and often hilarious book.

~ Pat and Peter Goodman
Motueka, New Zealand

This book is dedicated to three people in order of "who came first".

To my father, Alexander Patrick Horgan. A man much loved by his family and admired and respected by all who knew him, but none more than I.

To my brother Sean, my mentor and closest friend. (Until this is published!) No doubt he will vehemently deny any reference to his part in any of the stories!

Most of all however, to my wife Sue, who is, as always, totally supportive of my dreams and goals.

contents

III

maps

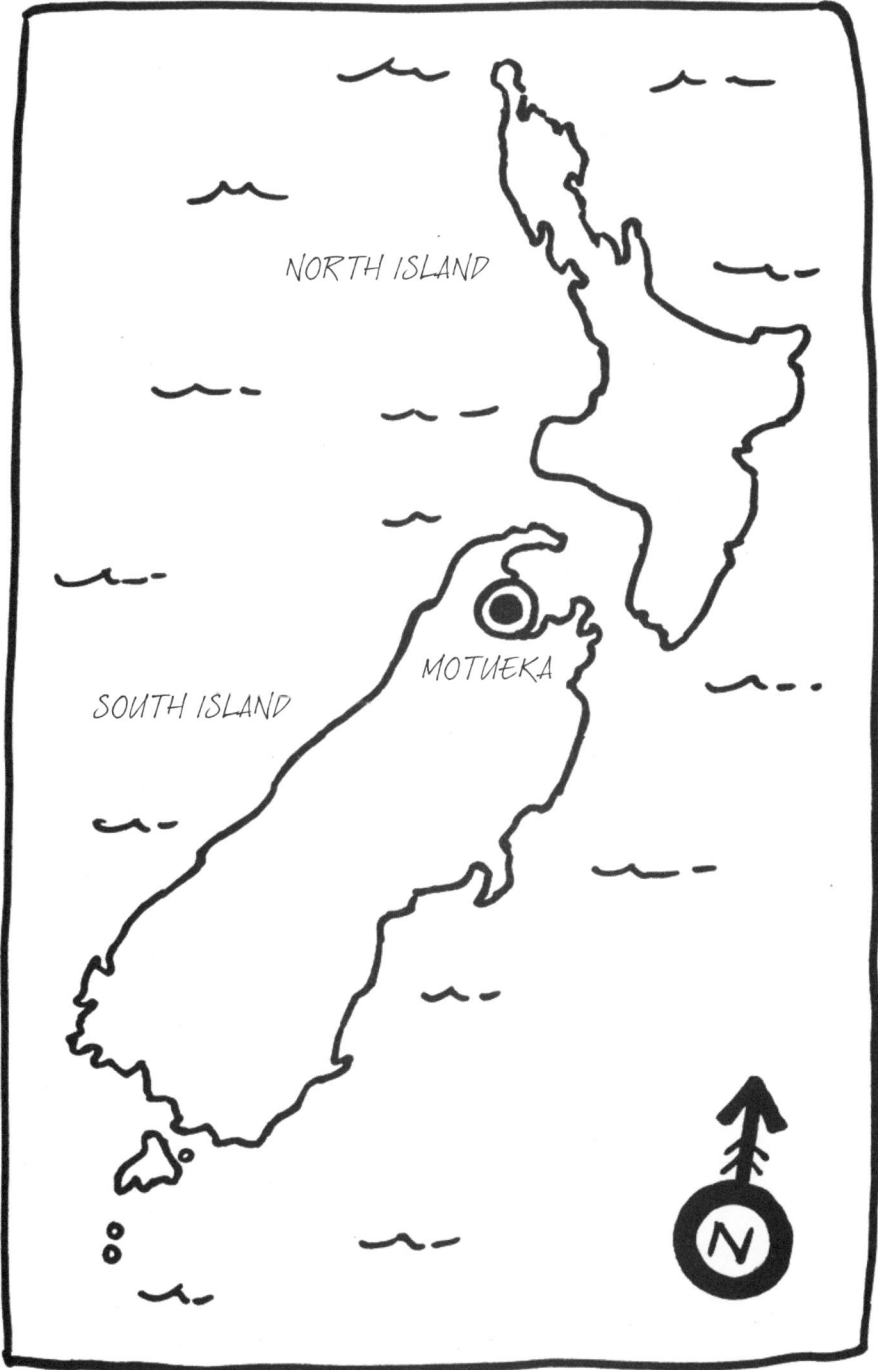

NORTH ISLAND

SOUTH ISLAND

MOTUEKA

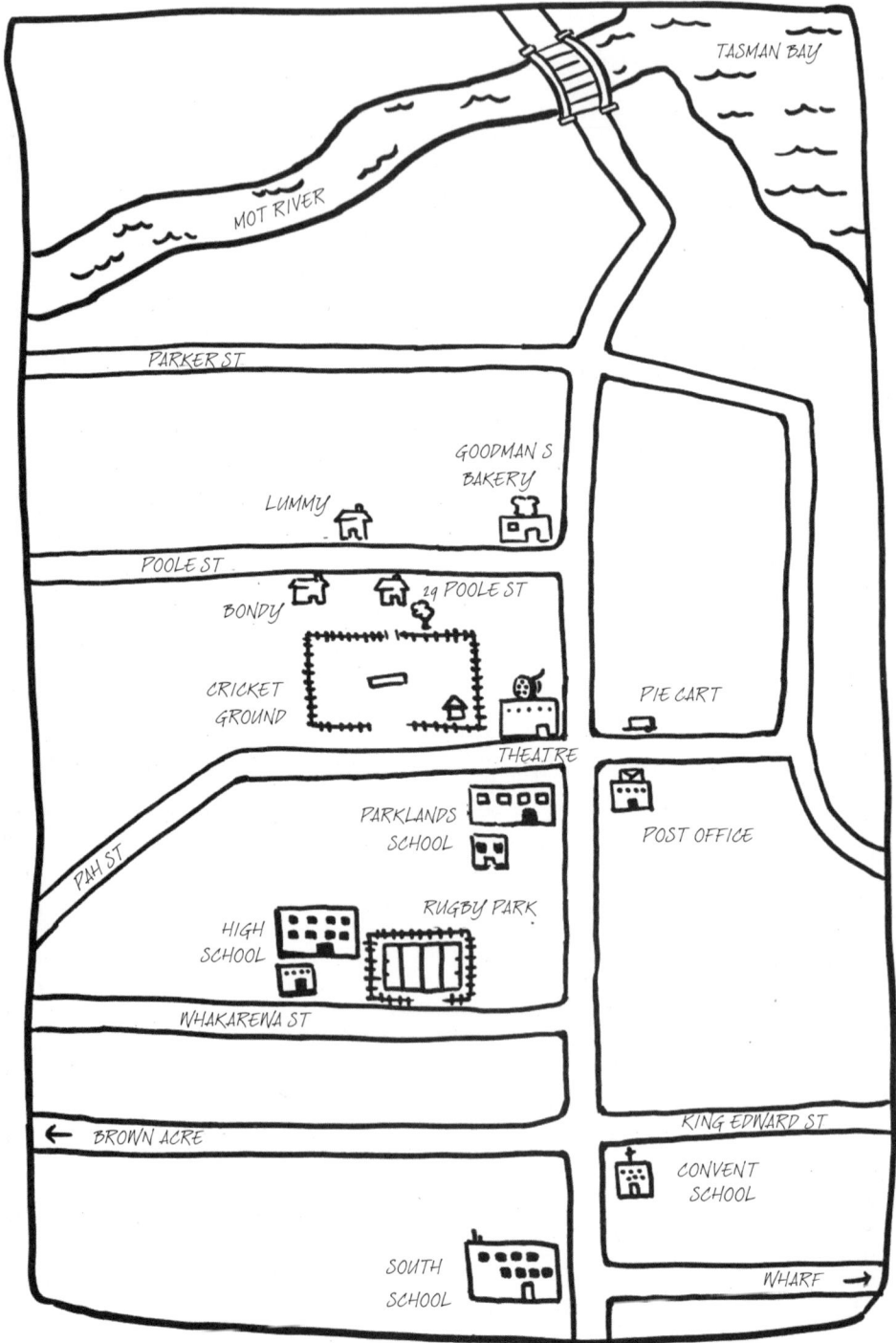

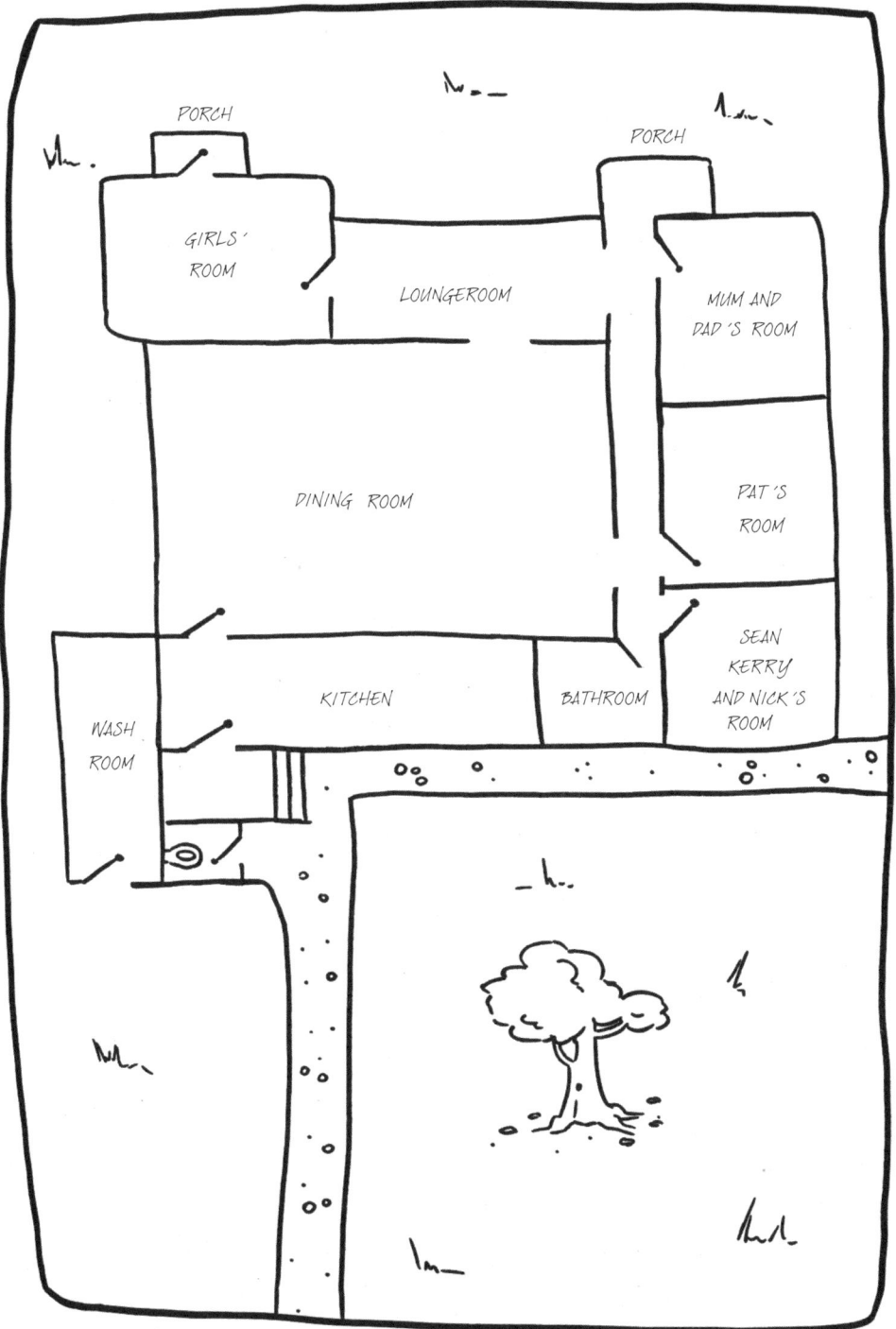

Introduction

AT THE END OF OUR STREET ....

... was a small bakery owned by Mr Ledger Goodman.

I was a little under four years old when I first visited the bakery on my own. It was barely a three-minute trike ride from our house. That day is still fresh in my mind. I parked the trike at the front door and just wandered into the bread shop at the front of the building and out into the bakery beyond.

Old Mr Goodman grabbed me with two big floury hands, each half covered with a square of rough-cut flour sack. He hoisted me up under the armpits and sat me on a huge sack of flour. From there I sat and watched proceedings in the warmth of the bakery whilst outside it was a typical Motueka clear and crisp spring morning.

The squares of flour sack on Mr Goodman's hands were makeshift gloves used for handling the hot bread tins and trays as he yanked them from the oven and placed them in cooling racks.

I vividly remember one of the bakers. I think his name was Bisley. He was mixing dough, and he had a "roll your own" smoke in his mouth. The ash was an inch long and it dropped into the dough. He looked up, winked at me, smiled, and kept on mixing.

Then Mr Goodman came over and gave me a round raisin bun onto which he had plastered white icing with some shredded coconut on the top. He dabbed some flour on my nose so that I would "look the same as him," he said. From then on, my visits to the bakery were frequent.

A few short years later, Goodmans built a new bakery. A "you beaut" one with New Zealand's first travelling oven. Pat and Peter Goodman, the sons of Ledger, would later go on to build one of the world's largest food companies from the base of this tiny bakery.

When I was nine years old, I was privileged to serve as an altar boy at the weddings of Pat, now Sir Pat, and Peter Goodman (whose knighthood is long overdue). Little did I know at the time, that I would spend twenty years of my adult life working for, and with, those two great men.

There are other success stories including the Talley brothers – Peter, Nicky and Michael. They took their father's small fish retailing business and turned it into one of New Zealand's largest fishing conglomerates. This business now employs a large percentage of Motueka's workforce.

This story has been written on the understanding that the incidents were fun at the time and never meant to hurt anyone. We were just kids, learning about life.

The background and upbringing, which we were so fortunate to have, has enabled all seven children of Jan and Alex Horgan to achieve a balance in later life, which I believe is the best. A place like the small town of Motueka gave us safety and freedom, and the understanding that our parents and the people of Motueka bestowed upon us, would prove to be the catalyst for our futures.

The people in this once tiny township, the "pearl" of New Zealand, either understood or turned a blind eye towards the Horgan kids and let us get away with unheard of stunts. They all played a part in expanding our horizons, which in turn was a major building block, enabling each one of us to eventually reach our goals and expectations. I do not suggest, however, this path for current or future generations, as times have changed, but it worked for us.

There were also other large families in the Motueka area with children our own age. Many of these kids remain close friends today and like us, are scattered around the world. They too, will have stories such as mine to tell, I'm sure.

My brothers and sisters — Pat, Hilary, Sean, Kerry, Veronica and Frances — and I spent our pre-teens and youth in Motueka, growing up in the '50s and '60s with Bill Haley, Buddy Holly, Elvis Presley, The Beatles, and the man who influenced them all, Chuck Berry. Others tagged along: Ricky Nelson, The Everly Brothers, Roy Orbison, The Rolling Stones, Bob Dylan, The Searchers and many more.

No cars for hooning, no drugs, no television until our mid-teens, no I-pods or computer games, and almost twenty years with no wars to fight in or worry about. In hindsight, it was about as fortunate a period as any child could get. It was a special time in history.

Although three of our family still live in the Province of Nelson, none lives in the town of Motueka. Probably just as well, if this manuscript ever goes to print.

We visit often and all still regard the town and its people the best of the best. Until the late 1960s, it seemed the town never grew. Few new people came to settle there during those years. It was quite isolated and in hindsight again, that was good. Now when I visit, I barely recognise the people except for long time friends and families in the district and yet to me it is still the small town of "Mot", our town. I do not seem to see the changes, and still see it the way it was during my childhood and teenage years.

The individual stories are a selection from a list that stretches over a period of twenty-four years, the last of which, ends the book – the day my mother passed away. I have tried to write from a "child's eye view" for many of the stories, especially the ones pre and early teen. I find it interesting when reading the final draft in that I think I actually captured the writing style of my teenage years. I felt I should change the style as I thought the publisher's editor would anyway.   Instead I left it as written and it stayed that way. The odd expletive, or, as I refer to it, "adjective", or as the nuns would say, "describing word", has been used to reinforce effect and not for any other reason.   God help us if we even thought of those words while still at home. A couple of names have been changed to protect the guilty!

I started preparing for this book some twenty years ago. At the time, I was advised to read as many books as I could before even attempting to write my own and so I did. Our current library consists of nearly three thousand books, on all sorts of topics, from gardening to mystery fiction. This has probably confused me more and has been the reason the book has taken me so long. I have made so many changes and rearrangements and strangely enough, I have now reverted to much of the original manuscript. I probably would have been better off reading a dictionary or thesaurus.

Thankyou, Motueka.

Earliest Memory

My earliest childhood memory is the trip to Motueka. Dad and Mum had accepted some sort of a promotion in the Post Office. We were moving from a town called Cheviot on the central east coast of the South Island of New Zealand, to another small town called Motueka, almost at the northern tip of the South Island.

We did not realise that we were moving from a pretty average town to one of the best small towns in the world. I was too young to know this at the time.

I was not yet two years old and we were travelling in the back of a Land Rover with a canvas canopy. It had flexible plastic windows in the canvas and these were so scratched and yellowed that you could not see through them. The back canvas panel was attached to the side panels with rope threaded through brass eyelets. The canopy covered the roof, sides and back of the vehicle. It was supported with an alloy frame.

I remember the scent of the Land Rover. It was one no other car had. Even Land Rovers today have that same distinctive smell. My brother Sean untied the canvas binding rope a few inches and lifted the flap. We looked from the back right hand corner of the Land Rover out across the Pacific Ocean as we drove along the coast road just north of a small town called Kaikoura. The moon reflected on the calm Pacific Ocean. I remember the stars in the clear night sky and the smell of the salt laden air. I will never forget it.

We were travelling with a friend of Mum and Dad's and were two hours into our six hour road trip to Motueka. Dad had gone ahead, travelling in the truck with our furniture. Another chance for him to get away from screaming and carsick kids! One of many chances he would jump at over the next few years.

I was too young to remember anything about the town where I was born. Cheviot was an hour and a half's drive north of Christchurch. Mum did tell us a bit about the town but it was so small that all she could tell us was exactly that. My godfather, Dave Costello, had a sheep station a few miles out of the town and apparently Dad and Dave used to do a bit of pig hunting in the Cheviot Hills, and a bit of boozing in the Cheviot pub. No doubt a lot more of the latter. Mum spent four years in Cheviot with my oldest brother and sister while Dad was gallivanting around Italy and Crete from 1941 to 1944.

Dad often said he was pretty pissed about the timing of the war. Aside from his Post Office career, he had played rugby union on Saturdays and rugby league on Sundays, being paid for league and not for rugby. He was also involved in professional sprinting. (Sprinting and high jumping would be a "way out" for us kids in later years!) He was the Canterbury sprint champion and an All Black trialist like his father.

In 1939, Dad was selected to play rugby league for New Zealand and was to tour England. Instead, the tour was cancelled and he got to tour Europe with the army! He got his tour of Europe all right but not playing league. The league tour had been cancelled courtesy of a bloke called Hitler and Dad's tour was behind a 303 Lee Enfield rifle. Quite amazing really, that Dad and all five of his brothers served in Europe during that war and all came home unscathed. Dad's sister was also in the air force. The worst injury any of them received was in two separate incidents – Dad being bitten by a scorpion out in the desert while trying to find Rommel. Hurt a bit he reckoned. Especially the second time!

In 1901, Dad's father was the first person in the world to jump six feet in an international sports tournament. His new record was six feet and one eighth of an inch. In those games, he won the high jump, long jump and the triple jump and one of my brothers has those gold medals today. To jump six feet in the high jump event in those days was no mean feat. The athletes ran straight at, and scissor stepped or simply leapt over the bar. There was no "western roll" or "Fosbury flop" back in 1901.

Grandad came to stay one day and as it happened, we had erected two tomato stakes, placed about five feet from each other, hammered into the ground. Each stake had nails banged into it at one-inch intervals from the two foot off the ground mark. A beanpole was perched on corresponding nails on each stake. We had marked each of the nail points in feet and inches. The highest we could jump was two feet eleven inches. Grandad walked over to where we were practising our high jump. He stood right alongside the horizontal bar and with no run up, jumped it! We were shattered. He was "really old" and what he had just done was impossible! I can still see the old coot jumping over the bar, dressed in his heavy woollen suit, tie and waistcoat. That was also the day he took a short length of rope in his teeth and Sean, Kerry and I held on to the dangling end of it. He then lifted all three of us off the ground and walked across the lawn, up the back steps and into the kitchen with us still hanging off the rope.

Bloody old show off, but what a couple of party tricks he had!

Paint

Dad had built us a playhouse under the pear tree. One Sunday he got a gallon of cream coloured, oil based enamel paint and "gave the playhouse a lick", as he would say. He planned to return the following day after work to give it a second lick!

For that reason he left the tin of paint, a screw driver and a couple of brushes along with half a gallon of turpentine in the playhouse. My sister Veronica was three and I was four, and on Monday after lunch, we discovered the paint. We decided to finish the job for Dad. We screw-drivered off the lid, just like Dad did. Then we took turns dipping the brushes in the tin and painted the walls, floor, window and ourselves. Yes hair, arms, faces and clothes – two coats each.

Mum discovered us two hours later. We had paid a visit to the sand pit after the paint job and had then tried to use the hose to wash off some of the sandy paint. It didn't work and we were now human sand paper.

I can still see the look on Mum's face. This was one of the stunts that really stumped her. She had previously reckoned she had "seen it all before". She just stood there. Hands on hips, lips pursed tightly in an exaggerated style as only she could do, trying to figure if it was our fault or Dad's for leaving the paint there. Or was it her fault for not keeping a closer eye on a three and four year old whilst at the same time attending to five year old Kerry who was sick in bed and had been for months, and keeping the baby, Francie, happy? Her mind was on overload trying to figure out what to do next.

She hauled us into the bathroom and sat us in the bath, where our bums stuck to the enamel. She fetched the half-gallon tin of turpentine. We were in for it now! It took her about four hours to get most of the paint off.

My hair was cut off in big chunks, not so delicately, as Mum was well into one of her famous "mute modes". This was when she was fed up and had had enough. She would stop talking, purse her lips and make a gesture with her hand as though she was slitting her throat. Her mute modes lasted anywhere from a few minutes up to days at a time. Pretty radical I thought.

Veronica had long thick blond hair and this day it had been in plaits. It had to go.

Worst of all the turpentine stung like hell and dried out our skin and boy, on your bum and private parts, nothing can describe the pain. Mum didn't seem to care. She was bawling, we were bawling, Francie was screaming out from her cot for no reason at all, but that was normal, and Kerry was yelling out for his medicine from the room next door. All in all, a hell of a commotion.

Mrs Crisp from the house next door obviously heard the yelling, bawling, screaming, and came running over to our house, in through the back door and into the bathroom. She saw Mum with her big dressmaking shears cutting off Ronk's hair and must have thought we were being murdered. She fainted immediately and fell to the bathroom floor.

Mum ran to the phone on the wall in the hallway. It was a phone where you left the receiver on the hook and wound the little handle. You then lifted the receiver and hoped like hell that someone in the telephone exchange would stop either gossiping or eavesdropping, answer it and then connect you to where you wanted to go. The exchange operators did this by pulling out a plug and shoving it into one of a million holes in a big board on the wall.

Mum was trying to call Dad at the Post Office, which was on the ground floor below the telephone exchange. For some reason most of the operators at the exchange eavesdropped whenever they could. If you wanted to know anything about anyone in Motueka, all you had to do was bribe or sleep with an operator. I once heard Dad say this to one of his mates in the pub! He was only kidding I'm sure. Knowing all of this, Mum and Dad had devised a code only they knew which would keep us free from the local gossip. It was apparently a simple single code word. I never knew what it was and only knew that there was such a code when Dad told me many years later as we were chatting over a game of crib.

Anyway, Dad got the call from Mum and ambled home to find the local police sergeant, the traffic cop and the doctor there already. He also learned that there was an ambulance on the way from Nelson, a city some thirty miles away. God knows who had arranged that.

All these people were jammed into our tiny bathroom and Mrs Crisp was now sitting up leaning against the wall waiting for her husband, Jack, to come and get her. Dad took one look at the scene and decided that there was nothing he could do except remember to buy some more paint and turpentine. He then buggered off to the pub with the police sergeant and the fat traffic cop. There they would discuss more important things such as rugby and trout fishing. Mum seemed to have it all under control, "in her own way", as usual.

Apparently, one of the gossiping eavesdroppers in the telephone exchange had arranged all the special services, none of which was required as far as we were concerned. All Ronk and I were doing was trying to help the old man out with his painting and it got slightly out of control.

Something we did learn from the episode was that the best way to get rid of a cat from your sand pit was to throw some turpentine on its bum. It will reach speeds of around fifty miles an hour. From then on, we just left the empty turpentine tin by the sand pit. At the mere sight of the tins, cats would even better the fifty mph speed and we never had problems with their poo in our pit from then on.

Talking About Hair

About a month after the body-painting episode, I was at my best mate's house, helping him wreck some of his toys. I picked up one of those little toy helicopters with a clockwork mechanism that, when you brush the wheels along the floor a couple of times, winds up a spring. This not only activates the rotor blades but also makes the wheels go round. You are then supposed to place the toy on the ground and away it goes on its merry way, blades spinning and wheels turning. Sometimes these toys had a flint system in them which sent out a shower of sparks.

If you want to do what I did that day, be prepared to run for it or get a hell of a hiding from the other kid's mother. I revved the heck out of the helicopter's wheels on the carpet and for some strange reason, lifted it in the air pretending that it could also fly. My arm took it in a loop and I landed it on my mate Michael's head. I honestly didn't do it on purpose. It just seemed a sort of a natural softish landing place!

Before the landing, Michael had a great head of thick, brownish, curly, hair. The clockwork type mechanism inside the helicopter was exposed on the underside of the toy. The innards of the toy's mechanism were a mass of interlocking wheels, steel bands and cogs. These sucked in great wads of Michael's curls in about a second flat. Not only that, the mechanism kept on going and the only way to stop the thing was to let it wind down.

At this stage, Michael was tearing around the lounge, screaming and bawling his head off, and the helicopter was gouging out big chunks of hair. He was trying to pull the bloody thing off his head but that was only making things worse.

Then his old lady came tearing into the room and cuffed me around the ear in her flying plight to get to Michael. I thought, shit how did she know it was me. Reputation I supposed!

Both Michael and his mother were trying to get the thing off his head but their hands were taking a battering from the rotor blades and still more of Michael's hair was being sucked up into the clockwork mechanism. The helicopter and his mother's hands were scalping poor Michael. Even I could have told them not to try to pull the thing off his head, but I was in shock, or probably awe, just to see the power of the little plane!

The helicopter finally ground to a halt on Michael's head. It looked quite funny actually, I thought, as I scampered out the back door to get my bike and get the hell out of there. On the way out the gate I swiped a handful of their *blue diamond* plums and hurled them over my shoulder onto their roof in retaliation for the whack around the ears!

Michael wore a hat to school for about two months after that. It seemed to take ages for his hair to grow back. It was weird to see Michael in church on the following Sundays with his hat on. Only girls were supposed to do that.

Michael went away to boarding school not long after that. I next ran into him in Christchurch when we were in our mid-twenties. He was about six foot six inches tall. I decided immediately not to mention helicopters as we reminisced.

The House At 29 Poole Street

Our home at 29 Poole Street was never tidy. Mum never had time for that sort of thing. The place was clean but there was stuff for miles. I recall a day during the May school holidays in 1966 when my brother Kerry, aged seventeen at the time, as a joke put a sign up at our front gate which read:

"FOR SALE. 1940 VACUUM CLEANER."
"MINT CONDITION."
"OFFERS"

The vacuum cleaner was twenty-six years old and Dad reckoned it had been used only twice. Once when the sales representative sold it to them and demonstrated it to Mum. The second time was when Mrs Crisp next door had borrowed it in 1956!

WHERE WILL YOUR TASTE BUDS

Whittaker's
SINCE 1896

TRAVEL NEXT?

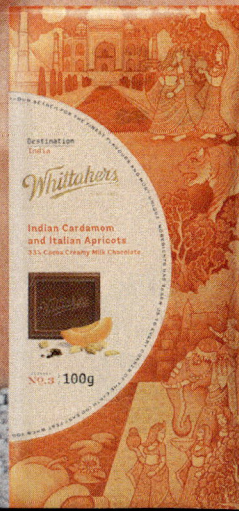

DELICATESSEN

t Cooked Chicken Size 16
cludes Free Range)

SUPER SAVER

11⁹⁹ ea

Choose from our delicious varieties instore!

Free Farmed Shaved Ham

1⁹⁹ 100g

Biersticks/Chorizo/Pepperoni

2⁹⁹ 100g

armland Ham & Chicken Luncheon/
ountry Pride Shaved Leg Ham 200g

SUPER SAVER

2 for 6⁰⁰

Farmland Ham & Chicken LUNCHEON
Original Like it used to be
Shaved Leg Ham
96% FAT FREE
GLUTEN FREE

USE BY

Roast Beef/Corned Silverside

1⁸⁹ 100g

Country Style Potato Salad

1⁷⁹ 100g

Whitestone Windsor Blue Wedge 110g

Club Deal

6⁹⁹ ea

ARTISAN CHEESE FROM OAMARU
NORTH OTAGO, NEW ZEALAND

WHITESTONE CHEESE CO
Windsor Blue
Delicate creamy blue
Soft texture
Silky smooth finish
Unique blue culture

WHITESTONECHEESE.COM

NZ Specialty Cheese

Massimo's Bocconcini/
Mozzarella 125g

5⁹⁹ ea

HANDCRAFTED IN NEW ZEALAND
SILVER MEDAL 2015
100 YEAR OLD RECIPE
MASSIMO'S BOCCONCINI

HANDCRAFTED NEW ZEALAND
ANIC
SILVER MEDAL 2014
100 YEAR OLD RECIPE
MASSIMO'S MOZZARELL

NZ Specialty Cheese

Although untidy inside, 29 Poole Street was home to anyone who didn't have one, for anyone who had one and didn't want to be there, and anyone who had been on the piss with Dad at the Post Office Hotel!

I was never embarrassed about the shambles the place always seemed to be in, that was just the way it was. Don't get me wrong however, the house was always clean, just untidy. Clean washing littered the lounge and dining room and I often remember the parish priest coming to visit. He always had to shift a pile of washing from a chair so that he could sit down.

A single large room served as both the kitchen and dining room. In the centre of the room, there was an oval oak dining table. It could seat all nine of us and by inserting two "leaves" or extensions in the centre of the table it could accommodate all of our family plus a couple of guests. Hands and faces had to be thoroughly washed and dried before we could even think about sitting at the table. Inspections were mandatory and generally carried out by Mum. We then sat at our nominated places. Sean, Kerry and I sat to Dad's left along the side of the table. Our chairs were against the wall and so there was no way we could escape in a hurry if things got difficult. We would have to sit and face the music.

One of us would be selected to say grace and then, and only then, could we start our meal. The other general rule was that "we could speak only when spoken to." To enforce the rules Dad had a bamboo cane, about four feet long, propped up in the corner behind his chair at the head of the table. Every now and again, when things got out of control, the old man would whip out the cane. He'd whack it down on the table barely inches in front of our dinner plates. Sean, Kerry and I would lurch to the left as Dad swung the cane. Mum's ESP came into action and to counter Dad's swipe, she would threaten us with an arm slap. We would all lurch back to the right. Just like three budgies on a swing!

Eventually Dad was bound to whack us with the cane or smash a plate or two in the process. Then he'd be in real deep shit with Mum. We thought drastic action was needed. So one day Sean took the cane out into Dad's shed and made about thirty, evenly spaced, saw cuts in it. The next night at dinner we made sure that the cane came out. When Dad whacked it on the table it flew into thirty-one pieces! There was deadly silence and Mum, and then Dad, burst out laughing. The next night Dad came in to dinner and as he sat he placed a thick black leather belt in front of his table setting and said nothing. Sean piped up and said, "Borrow it from the nuns did you?"

Not long after that Mum and Dad had to attend a meeting in the town. They asked the then fifteen-year-old Dennis Crisp, from next door, to baby-sit the five Horgan kids. Our older brother and sister, Pat and Hilary, had left home, one headed for the army and the other had her sights on becoming a dental nurse. Shades of Nurse Vondersmidt I thought! (Refer Chapter 11.)

Dennis decided that we should all play the board game Monopoly. The game was moving along quite smoothly until someone, me I think, decided to get up on the table on hands and knees to move his own marker. Someone else decided that I should not do this and got up on the table from the opposite side. You guessed it the table broke in half! Dennis was in for it now, we all blurted out. Mum loved that oak table.

Dennis chased us all off to bed and in the morning we found that he had propped the table up with a couple of wooden apple boxes. Dennis got the blame for the broken table in a five on one vote and was never asked back to baby-sit.

The kitchen was always full of a mix of clean and dirty dishes and cutlery. It was this way because Mum was always cooking meals and baking her famous scones, cookies and cakes. The oven was always on and the coal range, always on fire! It had a mind of its own.

Mum seemed to be an expert at most things except house tidiness and seven kids did not exactly assist in that art. The things she was expert in were cooking, gardening, having kids and bringing them up, talking, and her famous Mute Mode, when she got the shits!

Dad used to catch hundreds of trout each season as the Motueka River was trout heaven. Mum could cook them about a hundred different ways. We never bought vegetables. Mum and Dad grew them all and taught us how to do the same.

Looking back, the long list of fruit and vegetables we grew was amazing. There were three varieties of spuds, peas, beans, kumara, artichokes, tomatoes, lettuce, cauliflower, silver beet, cabbage plus many more.

Gooseberries, cape gooseberries, grapes, rhubarb, red and black currants, walnuts, peaches, apricots, plums, lemons, pears, boysenberries, raspberries, logan berries and even peanuts.

We had chooks and plenty of eggs and always had fresh fish from the bay, which we often caught ourselves. Then of course there were whitebait, before, during and after the season!

Strangely enough, we never had a fridge until 1957. Mum used to make all of our jams, pickles and preserves and had more bottled fruit than a modern day supermarket.

We never went hungry and nor did anyone else who just happened to drop by. Invited or not, they were always welcome at 29 Poole Street, the home of Jan and Alex Horgan.

The Sand Pit

Not long after Ronk and I painted ourselves, I found myself sitting in a pile of sand, we called our sand pit. A cubic yard of sand dumped on a sheet of flat iron. I was four years old and I had a plastic spade and bucket. I shared the sand pit with old cat shit, surrounded by the recently added empty turpentine tins. All of a sudden, the whole world seemed to turn upside down and the sand pit seemed to float. It was like my perceived view of what a ride on a magic carpet would be. Up until then I loved the stories about magic carpets. The earthquake changed it all.

It was two o'clock in the afternoon and we were seventy miles from the earthquake's epicentre. It registered over six on the Richter scale but probably only half of that in Motueka. It was an experience I will never forget and over the next few years, I would never get used to the earthquakes, which occurred at least once a year.

I remember the stories of how during the Murchison earthquakes of 1929, there were over 170 earthquakes recorded in the hills behind Motueka. These, in a period of four months – July through October. The quakes continued through until April the following year. Some of these quakes lasted for thirty minutes or so: the longest was said to have lasted for forty-five minutes. I found that amazing! Even more amazing that the South Island still exists!

I never went near the sand pit again and still have a phobia about walking on sand at the beach!

New Bikes

I started school a year after my brother Kerry and was only at the state primary school for a year until the new Catholic convent school opened. The state primary school had been only a couple of hundred yards away across the park within easy walking distance from our house.

Unfortunately for Dad, the convent school was more than a mile from our house and so he had to find some bikes for us in a hurry. He then had to teach us how to ride them. Kerry had been fairly sick for a while and so he got a brand new Raleigh sports bike. From the day he got the bike a miracle occurred and he recovered from his illness! I got a little second hand mongrel but it was a bike and that's all that mattered.

Dad had a third job in those days and from February until Easter he would be off picking fruit or tobacco most weekends. This year it paid for the new bikes.

Catholics rarely worked on Sundays, except for Dad but he did attend early mass first! Because he worked Saturdays and Sundays picking apples, tobacco or whatever, he had little time to teach us how to ride our bikes. He only had about ten minutes left at seven o'clock on Monday morning before our first day at the new convent school.

The street had recently been very roughly surfaced with tar and embedded with very sharp quarry stone. Until a few months before, the town had either been on septic tanks or the houses had short drop dunnies down in the back garden. Each of these short drop dunnies had a can placed about a foot below the seat. At night when we were asleep the "night man" would come around, get the can, tip the contents into a big bin on the back of his old truck and then deposit it somewhere. I never saw the "night man" and never found out who he was. Not that I really cared! As a matter of interest, a big coal truck hit the "night truck" early one morning down in the main street. Talk about Shit Street!

Anyway, the council decided to put the whole town on a sewer system and with this, all the streets were consequently re-sealed. When new sewer systems were installed in those days a huge ditch digger would dig a trench from one end of the street to the other. For months there was a resident crater in our street. The sewer and resurfacing were being addressed in sections of about three hundred yards. Each of these seemed to take months to complete. Our street was attacked in the wintertime. More often than not the crater would fill with water and would have to be pumped out before more work could be done. During that time the street was a four-foot deep lake. We used to build canoes and makeshift boats and have heaps of muddy fun, much to Mum's annoyance.

Dad took Kerry and me out onto the street with our new bikes. In 1955 there were no such things as bike helmets, chain guards or training wheels. Dad sat us on the seats of our respective bikes. He told us that to stop we had to either jump off, ride into a bush, or apply the back pedal brakes and we would simply fall over. I favoured the bush alternative.

With a hand under the back of each bike seat and standing in between us, he slowly extended both bikes at arm's length behind him. Like winding up and then unleashing two rubber bands, he quickly propelled us forward down the street. At the same time he yelled, "Ride or die!"

We rode!

When our younger sisters Veronica and Francie started school, Kerry and I had to double them. To double someone meant that the "doublee" sat side-saddle on the cross bar of the bike. This was a horizontal bit of steel tube, which ran from the front forks to a point under the seat. You could not double on a woman's bike because there was no horizontal tube connecting the seat to the front forks. Instead, there was a "V" put there so that girls could ride bikes with a dress on I suppose.

For blokes, riding a lady's bike was a bit more hazardous than riding a man's bike. If the chain broke, a foot slipped off a pedal when you were riding in the standing position, or if the chain came off because it was too loose, you would drop about two feet into the slot of the "V". Shit it was a painful experience. If the chain broke on a man's bike, you did not drop so far but it still hurt like hell when your crotch connected with the horizontal bar. In either case, you would also stub your toes on the roadway because most of the time you were bare footed.

One particular morning my bike had a flat tyre and because we were running late, as usual, there was no time to mend the puncture. We decided that all four of us would ride to school on Kerry's bike, at the same time! To start off, we placed two apple boxes on the ground on either side of the bike and loaded ourselves on board.

Kerry rode the bike, I sat on the bar, Francie sat straddling the carrier above the back wheel. Veronica sat on the handlebars facing forward, and we were off. We had practised this stunt heaps of times and although there were a few pitfalls, you could pull it off reasonably easily. One pitfall was that the person on the carrier could not let her dress get caught either in the rear sprocket or in the back wheel spokes. Therefore, Francie had to sit there with her skirt tucked up under her bum and her feet held high and wide, like flying!

For me as the "doublee", the bar was the safest position. However, I had nothing to hold on to because Veronica was sitting on the handlebars in front of me, my normal handhold if there were only two of us on the bike. Therefore, I had to hold on to either her shoulders or hair in which case she dare not move.

Veronica's position on the handlebars was also fairly hazardous in that her weight (not that she was that fat – just dumpy) made turning the handlebars fairly tricky. If she did not sit still the front wheel could jack knife. This caused all sorts of problems, not to mention her losing a fist full of hair! She would sit with her bum on the handlebars with the head light between her thighs. She held onto the handlebars on either side of her bum. Her feet could also be a big problem if either one got anywhere near the front wheel spokes. This would end in all of us doing a mighty somersault. Her feet were sticking out at a forty-five degree angle. The bike looked like it was made of kids with two sets of wings.

Off we went down Poole Street passing Goodman's bakery on the left and then turning right at the T intersection with High Street. We were lucky there were no cars coming when we turned as I doubt if we could have stopped in time to avoid a collision.

Four kids on a bike, which had gears, could gather quite a momentum and stopping would be a bit of a trick when we arrived at school later on. It was made even more precarious as none of us could touch the ground with our feet while on the bike. Our plan was for Kerry to steer the bike's front wheel into the slots of the bike stand where we hoped it would hold long enough for us all to jump off.

The township proper started as we turned to the right, with shops either side of the street. These continued down High Street for the next half mile or so. The shops actually started with Goodman's bakery on one side of the street and a pub on the other. There was another pub in the centre of the town and a third at the end of the shops. Then the houses began again.

We were riding along quite merrily when about two hundred yards down

High Street we spotted a mate, Piers Lummis or "Lummy", standing on the other side. Even though Lummy was a Protestant, and went to the state school, he was a good mate. He lived with his Grandma just a few houses down from us on the other side of our street.

We all saw him at the same time while clipping along at a rapid speed. All four of us were yelling greetings and waving furiously. So was Lummy for a short while, and then he seemed to be pointing ahead of us and yelling something back. We couldn't hear what he was saying and we certainly didn't see the taxi, one of only two in Motueka. It had stopped directly in front of us.

Miss Ingram, a teacher at the state primary school, was getting out of the rear passenger door of the taxi. She was an overly largish woman and her bum was even larger and it was sticking out into the street. She was obviously reaching for her bag on the back seat and her head was still inside. The front wheel of the bike caught her right between the cheeks throwing her headfirst into the back of the taxi.

Veronica flew off the handle bars crashing into the open back door. Kerry and I followed. The back door got flattened one hundred and eighty degrees around into the front door. A split second later Francie followed us taking out the external rear vision mirror on Mr McGregor's near new, light green, Mark 1 Ford Zephyr taxi.

The four Horgan kids didn't know what hit them nor did Miss Ingram. People swarmed around trying to bandage our cuts and grazes. The front wheel of Kerry's bike was square and the handlebars bent sideways. The taxi door and side mirror were write offs. Through it all Mr McGregor sat in the driver's seat in total shock and dismay lamenting the condition of his near new car.

Lummy was pissing himself with laughter. We didn't think it was so funny until later, about a week later, when all the hubbub died down and the bruises had faded.

Miss Ingram, of the famed duo of "Black and Ingram", the state school primary teachers, (more on them later) was sprawled face down in the back seat. She had knocked herself out when she went head first into the rear left hand side window. Mr Budden, from Budden's bookshop, adjacent to the mishap, was trying to revive her with some smelling salts.

Mr Smith from Smith's Cycles bike shop had grabbed Kerry's bike in a flash, and half wheeled, half lifted it down the street to his shop for repairs. Like a bloody vulture (or a modern day tow truck operator) he grabbed the bike before his competitor in the town, Winn's Cycles, could get anywhere near the scene of the crime.

All four of us limped the rest of the way to school, egos dented and the wind literally knocked out of our sails, only to be beaten up by Sisters Gabriel and Philomena for being late! This pair of rosary beaded women in black tolerated not even reasonable excuses. Theirs was probably a lighter punishment than the one we would have received if we had still been attending Black and Ingram's state school primary classes. We had almost killed the local icon of teaching, and Prime Minister's sister, Miss Ingram.

She actually went on to get an OBE from the Queen and died aged about a hundred. Probably even got "the telegram" as well. In hindsight, the whack on the head obviously didn't affect her at all. May have even helped her achieve the ton!

Some Sundays

Some Sunday mornings after mass, Dad would take us on a bike ride from the church down Fearon Street where we would stop outside the fence of the best house in Mot. It belonged to a bloke called Mac Inglis. Mac grew hops, tobacco and also had a large dairy herd.

The house was set back on about four acres of gardens and in the centre of the beautifully manicured lawns was a huge fountain. At night it was lit up in all the colours of the rainbow. For the mid-1950s, this was quite incredible.

There was also a small lake, about an acre in size, and on it were ducks and some huge black swans. We used to feed them with scraps of bread. The swans were vicious brutes, however, and we found this out one night in the dark when a couple of us sneaked over the concrete fence. We raced across the gardens and emptied a carton of Mum's washing powder,

Lux Flakes, into the fountain. On the way back across the lawn we ran slap bang into a group of half a dozen very territorial and angry black swan watch dogs. They sure have a nasty peck. The next morning the fountain and lawns were a sea of froth, and we were a mess of bloodied pecks.

After we fed the ducks and swans, we'd continue our bike ride around the eastern outskirts of the town. We would stop at a little general store down at the Motueka beach where Dad would buy us an ice cream. That was a real treat.

That little shop is no longer there. The bloke that owned it when we were kids used to store empty lemonade bottles in a stack out the back of the shop, up against the wall. In those days, you got a refund of a penny for each empty beer bottle, threepence for small lemonade bottles and sixpence for large lemonade bottles. This shop was a perfect recycler for kids so it was rumoured. They would sneak around the back of the shop, collect half a dozen bottles, then take them around to the front of the shop, and get a refund!

Then we would continue on to the wharf. If the tide was in we would sit for an hour or even longer on the bollards and fish for herrings and the odd bream in the deep blue-green waters far below the wharf. There were always fishing trawlers berthed there and now and again a cargo ship.

Black and Ingram Vs Gabriel and Philomena (and Other Things!)

I started school aged five at the state public primary school.

"The school, later to be renamed Parklands, was situated out our back gate, across the cricket ground, across Pah Street, past the dreaded school dental clinic which housed the dreaded Nurse Vondersmidt, (the acting dental nurse whom I was to learn lots about later), across the grass playground where the Queen drove in a Rolls Royce convertible and waved to a "million" kids in 1955, or thereabouts, (I know because I was one of them), across the concrete tennis courts and finally into Miss Black and Miss Ingram's primary class." A daily ritual.

As you can imagine there were lots of attractions, some good and some bad, along the way. It was only a couple of hundred yards as the shanghai's stone flies, yet one could take all day getting there if one was allowed to. I hated the walk to school and I hated the class. I cannot even remember who took me there on the first day but if I ever find out, I'll kill them!

All the kids sat on their own little mat. Many of the kids had gone to kindergarten but not me, possibly because I still sucked my thumb. I did so until I was about eight.

I cannot remember what we did in class in the mornings but after lunch at one o'clock, for half an hour, we were forced at ruler point to "go to sleep or else" on our little mats. There we all were, feigning sleep with one eye closed and the other on the wall clock. I did not know how to tell the time at that stage. I sure knew, however, that when the big hand was in the straight up and down position and the little hand was half way between the two and the three, it was time to bolt.

"Across the concrete, over the grass, past the dental clinic, giving it as wide a berth as possible, across Pah Street, across the cricket ground and through our back gate where the real day could now begin." Another daily ritual.

A year or so after I started school, the new Catholic school opened and we were introduced to the Sisters of St Joseph, Gabriel and Philomena. Right from the start, Black and Ingram seemed a better bet in spite of the mats on the floor and the forced afternoon sleep. There must have been a bit of collusion between the four single women teachers regarding the "sleep thing". Although the nuns did not believe in the "mat thing" they did have the sleep thing on the curriculum. We had to fold our arms on the desks, rest our heads on our arms and pretend that we were sleeping for half an hour or so after lunch. This position was uncomfortable and virtually impossible to sleep in.

Sisters Gabriel and Philomena really enforced the sleep thing. They marched up and down the rows of desks with a ruler in each hand, belting any kid across the back of the head who dared lift their head or open their eyes. Fifty years later, these two could easily have got jobs as guards at Guantanamo Bay!

There were a few occasions when I pretended to go to sleep and feigned this for a couple of hours until it was time to go home. I was not on my own with this little trick but in hindsight, I reckon the nuns knew we were taking a loan of them. You could actually plan this however, by yawning through the classes during the morning and tearing around the playground during the lunch break, making sure the nuns noticed you. Then you pretended to sleep it off for a couple of hours after lunch.

I think the nuns and Black and Ingram were a bit silly forcing the half-hour sleep on us. They could have just booted us out of school half an hour earlier and all parties would have been more than happy.

The nuns were from the order of St Joseph. They were a good looking bunch of birds but then all we ever saw of them was their faces. Everything else was covered. How they must have sweltered in the summer heat. They had long dark brown habits which covered them from the top of their heads to their feet. They had white bands that covered their foreheads, cheeks and throat. I bet they got pimples under those things. Did they have hair or were they bald? They all looked like Darth Vader. I often sat in class and wondered what colour their hair was and what they wore when they went to the beach for a swim. When they got home from school in the late afternoon did they get their gear off and wander round in shorts, tee shirts and jandals? Did they ever sit out the back of their convent house and do a bit of sunbathing? I can just see them there lounging around with a six pack discussing what little bastards they had to put up with all day. In fact they probably could have dressed up in civilian clothes and buggered off to the beach on hot days with a pair of sunglasses on. No-one would have recognised them except for their bald heads, pimples and ultra white skin. They probably did! Who knows? It was all a mystery to me.

The classroom had a little round radio, which sat up on top of a bookcase. I will never forget it, because I was the poor bugger blamed for its demise in my final year of primary school. It was a perfectly round, dark brown bakelite, Phillips branded radio about eight inches in diameter. No wonder it rolled off the top of the bookcase all on its own! On Mondays after lunch, Sister Gabriel would ask the most senior pupil, usually Herman Roborgh, to turn it on and tune it to the national radio station. We would all then pretend to be riveted to *The World We Live In*. Half an hour of obsolete trivia.

We each had a new desk and chair at the convent school. Throughout the years I spent there, the chairs and desks remained as new as they were on day one, devoid of any scratches or marks. This was the result of the nuns' strict reign of terror. The threatened punishment for graffiti on anything anywhere was a mixture of an immediate hell of a hiding on earth, coupled with the threat of an extended stay in purgatory when we died.

If I had died at the end of my years at the convent school, I would still be in purgatory today some forty-five years later! Some of the things we did, and should not have done, included the fight with my best mate Michael Small. This ended up with us both crashing into a cabinet that was the base for a three-foot high statue of the Virgin Mary. Mary ended up on the floor in a million pieces.

When I got to the state high school, the desks and the chairs seemed to have the names of every kid who ever sat, etched into them. I even saw the names of some ex-convent school kids amongst them. Probably more ex-convent names than kids from the state primary schools simply because this was a new form of entertainment. At the end of every year, in the week after exams, the wood-working classes would have the job of sanding down the desktops. Then they re-varnished them in readiness for the start of school in February. The table legs and chairs had never been sanded. Some of the names on them went back to 1955 when the high school first opened.

The local priest at the time, "Brick Bradford", built Saint Peter Chanel's Catholic Convent Primary School. He fancied himself as a carpenter more so than a priest. As a priest, he was known for his long-winded fiery sermons on hell, but as a carpenter, he would be remembered for the school he built. Not necessarily by the kids who attended but by the community. In addition, Black and Ingram would have thanked Father Bradford many times, in particular, for taking the Horgan kids away from the state primary school.

Brick Bradford had a little mate, "Tonto", helping him, who really was a carpenter and was a Protestant to boot. These two were a strange combination. It was rare in those days for Catholics to hire non-Catholic contractors. It was rumoured however that Tonto was a wayward Catholic and perhaps Brick had told him that his reward would be heaven when he died. He is dead now and I wonder if he made it?

The school consisted of three classrooms. Two of them were used for classes and the other was the music room. It had a piano and one chair and absolutely nothing else. Not even a statue on a bookcase! Quite unusual for a Catholic school classroom but I guess that at the rate statues got smashed the nuns thought the better of putting one in an empty room. Perhaps the high-pitched voices of the kids' choir might shatter it.

When Brick Bradford had built the school, one of his final additions was to erect some pink marble slabs, sort of facades, at the front of the building between the walls separating each of the classrooms. The slabs were about a yard wide and four yards high. They would have weighed at least two tons each and the method of fixing them must have been a bit dodgy.

A few weeks after we started school at the convent, all forty-five of us were sitting on the concrete steps outside the classrooms having our lunch. We went to play and then went back to class. We had no sooner sat at our desks when there was a hell of a crash outside. One of the slabs had fallen from the wall and crashed into thousands of bits on the concrete steps where, just a short time before, we had all been sitting. Could have wiped out twenty percent of the school's population in one fell swoop!

Catholic schools received no subsidies or handouts from government in those days and the Catholic families also had to pay school fees. While many of these schools are now integrated into the State system, the Church has to maintain the property so Catholic schools still charge fees. It was tough on the families who were not financial.

The only thing the government did give us on a daily basis was forty-five half pint bottles of un-pasteurised warm milk. Each kid had to drink the stuff under threat of death! I still reckon that it was a conspiracy by the government to kill off all the Catholic kids. Or maybe the government was targeting kids in general as I had heard that our Protestant counterparts also had to drink the milk. In the summer time, there were no refrigerators and the milk curdled in the heat. During winter, for some mysterious reason, we used to have to stack the crates of milk by the fireplaces or by the heaters to warm it up! There were no excuses. The milk had to be drunk. Maybe there was some sort of a deal between the dairy farmers and the government. The revenue for half a million pints of milk a day would have been quite substantial. Those were the days when Dad and his mates used to drink warm beer as well but beer didn't curdle. There did not have to be any excuses for drinking the beer though, even when it was warm but it wasn't free like the milk!

We did not have a tennis court at the convent school but Parklands School did. In fact, they had four of them just outside Black and Ingram's primary class. One day during my first two weeks at school, it was playtime and we were playing soccer on one end of the concrete tennis courts. There were about a hundred kids on each team. The ball was booted out of bounds under the tennis net and I was after it. The net however, had previously been taken away for repair and the sagging wire that held the net in place was still there. No occupational health and safety issues in 1955! I connected with the wire losing three teeth in one hit. It hurt a bit. I have always hated tennis and I think that is why.

The Chiming Clock

It was a beautiful old wind-up chiming clock. It had been a present to Mum and Dad from the Post Office when Dad returned from the Second World War, and we moved up to Motueka from Cheviot in North Canterbury. Whether it was a present for getting home from the war or a bribe to get us out of Cheviot, I'll never know.

It sat in the centre of the mantelpiece above the fireplace in the lounge or "front room" as we called it. Some chiming clocks are as ugly as sin but this one was simple, yet elegant. Long in comparison to some, but not too long, and someone who was truly an artist had obviously designed it. There were three holes in the face and every few days Dad would haul out a huge key and wind it up. He would insert the key in each of the holes. The first was for the mechanism, the second for the chimes and finally a third keyhole was wound up. I never knew what the third keyhole was for and I don't think Dad did either.

On either side of the clock were various family trophies and cups won for flower shows, singing competitions and sports awards. There were also a few art treasures that Dad had sent to Mum during the war from places like Vienna.

I doubt if Kerry was five years old at the time when he reached up to get a peacock feather off the mantelpiece, or perhaps a sixpence that Dad had put there. He slipped and to steady himself he grabbed for the edge of the mantelpiece, which was at the height of his out-stretched hand. He then fell backwards hanging onto the felt that was under the clock. There was a hell of a crash as the clock and the rest of the paraphernalia came down around him onto the enamelled concrete hearth. The clock smashed into a million bits and as usual, Kerry bolted. So did I.

I can't remember how he explained that one away. He tried to blame me if I recall but that backfired on him because I could not yet reach the mantelpiece.

The clock was repaired, in time, (so to speak) but the chime was never the same and the time was always wrong. Dad still went through the motions of winding it up but I think it was just from habit. I don't know who the clock was bequeathed to either … probably Kerry!

Marbles

We had thousands of marbles and I don't recall ever buying any of them! They came in all sizes and colours. The smallest was about half an inch in diameter and the largest was approximately one and a half inches in diameter. The large ones were rarely used in the two main marble game variants, but rather, used in the "eye bombs" offshoot of these games.

The two games we generally played at school were traditional marbles and rounders. Any number of players played traditional marbles. A line was drawn across the concrete in chalk. Approximately ten feet from the chalk line was a hole in the concrete, a scoured out crack or a hole, the latter, which may have once housed a basketball hoop support pole. These holes were generally about two and a half inches in diameter.

Someone once told me that if I could describe the game of marbles I would be a genius, so the reader is asked to use a bit of imagination.

Each player would kneel on the chalk line and flick his marble at the hole. The initial aim was to get the marble into the hole in one shot. All the players had one flick to start the game. There are two or three styles of flick, but generally the forefinger is crooked and the thumbnail bent into the crook of the forefinger. The marble is then placed between the friction points of the connection. By releasing the thumb in a flicking motion, the marble is projected forward at a pace determined by the amount of pressure exerted by the thumb.

If no player makes the hole in one flick, all of the players have another flick in the same order. The first player to get a marble in the hole then has the opportunity to flick his marble at any of the other players' marbles. His flick position is from the hole itself. If he connects another player's marble then he claims the marble and pockets it. He then aims at another player's marble and if he misses, all the players, in turn, flick for the hole again. The owner/s of the marbles "claimed" are no longer in the game and have to sit it out until the next new game. The game is complete when there is one player and one marble left.

An unlimited number of players also play the game of rounders. Here a circle of about ten feet in diameter is drawn on the concrete. Another smaller circle of approximately two feet is drawn in the centre of the larger circle. Each player has two marbles, one of which is placed in the inner circle. Players take turns to flick their second marble from the edge of the outer ring at any of the marbles within the rings. The aim is to knock any other player's marble out of the diameters of the rings and then they may claim it. The player whose marble has been claimed stays in the game but to continue he must place another marble in the circle if he chooses to do so, or retire from the game. Any player whose turn comes up may target marbles anywhere within the circles. Each player has the right of continuous play until he misses knocking any given marble from the circles in successive flicks. Then the next player steps up. The game continues until there are no marbles left in the inner ring or within the outer ring.

In this version of the game, there is a second way to claim marbles from the centre and this is called "eye bombs". A player whose turn has come plays this by electing to eye bomb instead of flick. He simply takes the largest of his marbles, the inch and a half size and stands directly above any of the marbles in the inner circle. Holding his large marble on his cheek just below his eye, he lines up the target marble and drops it, hoping to hit the marble on the concrete. This is a lot more difficult than one would think. If he does connect and the target marble exits the outer circle, the player may claim it.

Rounders is a great game for sneaky little crooks and outright thieves. Most players have their favourite marble or "mig", treasured for the number of enemy marbles it has claimed. Favourites are often swapped for other marbles or quantities of other marbles. The "cat's-eye" was a favourite when we were at primary school. These were small, generally white, with a black or blue, opal coloured dot. Other players preferred the "Dutchie" because it was slightly larger than standard. It was made of clear glass and had different coloured leaf shaped flashes within the marble itself. These were far more common than cat's eyes.

Some players had a knack of claiming large amounts of marbles using their favourite mig. You couldn't beg borrow or steal them from their owners. The best way to take them out, however, was by eye bombing them. At the last moment before you dropped your inch and a half sized marble, you swapped it for a ball bearing of the same diameter. The ball bearings were easy to paint to resemble ordinary marbles. If your aim was good, you could shatter your opponent's favourite mig if they were silly enough to leave it in the circle. However, you had to be prepared to run for your life if the bloke who owned it was a bully or was bigger than you were! The trick to winning this game was a combination of three or four factors, the least of which was skill.

The marble season was in the summer time. Yes, unbelievably there was a marble season. Most kids wore sandals without socks to school in summer and these were often discarded in favour of bare feet, especially by some of the marble players. The more players involved in a game of rounders the better. There are not supposed to be teams as such but there were for us.

Our team consisted of a nominated player, a couple of "outriders" and a couple of "hangers-on." It took a bit of practice but imagine a dozen players on their knees around the outer circle playing the game with the supporters and onlookers standing behind them. In amongst these last two groups were your outriders and the hangers-on.

Our player was advised to play an average game. It was hoped that this would not bring undue attention. We claimed a lot more marbles that way, and were above suspicion of any sort of skulduggery. He would flick and miss and then all of the attention was on the next player. The new player would flick his marble into the centre scattering the marbles some of which would cannon off others and zoom outside the outer circle. Here the outriders would be yelling and shouting and creating all sorts of a commotion and in doing so, inciting the rest of the onlookers to do the same. At the same time, the bare feet of the outriders would stand on a marble or two. These can be easily wedged between toes. The knee is then bent up behind and the hand extracts the marble or marbles from the toes. The marbles are quickly palmed to the hangers-on who depart the scene and stash the pinched migs before returning to await the next opportunity. At this point, after much grumbling, the game continues. Lost marbles may be replaced by the "lossee." Every now and again, all the players agree to search the onlookers. A renegade marble was rarely discovered in a pocket where it should not have been!

At the end of the game, the outriders and the hangers-on return to the scene to mingle and commiserate with the players who lost marbles in mysterious fashion. I never could figure out why no one ever cottoned on to this simple but very effective swindle. It was effective and never-ending because at the Parklands School there were hundreds of kids and many games being played simultaneously.

The best day of the marbles season was "smugglers" day. This was a day when you could legally pinch as many marbles as you dared without being caught. If caught, marbles were forfeited. Our best smugglers day yielded almost 200 marbles! We never actually played the game on smugglers day. We just sort of mingled in the crowds of kids playing the games, uplifting marbles and bags of marbles wherever possible.

In the end, we had marble phobia. Then we had the problem of where to hide all the marbles. Hundreds and hundreds of them. We used to fill empty *Edmond's Baking Powder* tins with marbles and bury them in marked spots in the garden. We used them in our cattys and shanghais but still there were thousands left over. I wonder if subsequent residents of 29 Poole Street ever discovered our "marble graveyard."

The grand finale of our marble days came one stormy, rainy day. Due to the storm and promised flood, the schools were closed. We were bored at being cooped up in the house and needed something to amuse us. Dad was at work and Mum had a doctor's appointment.

This also turned out to be the day before all unburied marbles were ruthlessly hunted down by Charlotte Jeanne Horgan ("The Marble Crusades".) New marbles entering the site from that day onwards were totally banned under threat of death!

Mum had a beautiful oak breakfast tray. It was an antique and had ivory inserts inlaid into the silver handles at each end. It was only used to take meals to Dad in bed if he was ever ill, which was rare indeed. We decided that it would make a good toboggan if only it had wheels.

Some bright spark solved that issue by suggesting that we spread marbles the length and breadth of the hallway from the bathroom at one end to the front door entrance at the other. The plan was then to sit the oak tray on the marbles and by tying a thin rope to the handle on one end, we could pull each other up and down the hallway. The rope was about thirty yards long. It extended from the toboggan, down the hall, out the front door and over the verandah. It then went down a couple of steps and through the eye of a pulley that Sean had found in the shed. He tied the rope and pulley to the verandah handrail for extra leverage, and then it ran out onto the soggy front lawn.

I don't know who got the first ride but it was probably Sean as he was the oldest of the "post war" Horgans. He sat on the tray on the bed of marbles while the rest of us stood in a line on the front lawn. Like a tug-of-war team, we took off at great speed across the lawn with Sean in tow.

He zoomed down the hallway and literally flew over the veranda and landed on the soggy grass with a thump. We were all laughing and rolling around in a heap in the hydrangea bushes in the garden off the edge of the lawn. What fun. We all had a couple of turns. The second turn was at extra speed. Sean had decided that if we tied the end of the rope to one of our bikes and used another pulley one of us could roar down the driveway. This worked well and before long, we were riding two up on the toboggan. Then the handle with the rope attached came adrift so we turned the tray around until the other handle was buggered.

The hallway ended up a mess of broken and crushed glass marbles. The skirting boards along the bottom of the walls, below the wallpaper were all scarred and scratched. That was not so much of a problem compared to the underside of Mum's treasured oak tray. It was scored and scarred with awesome grooves made by the marbles. The handles were long gone!

Then Mum arrived home. We hurriedly hid the tray and began to sweep up all the whole and partial marbles and tiny bits of glass that littered the hallway. Mum caught us in the act during the cleanup but did not notice the tray, or what was left of it!

Unbelievably, the next morning Dad was sick. Mum scoured the place for the oak tray and let out a hell of a shriek when she finally found it. Dad came running from his sick bed and we all bolted for the safety of the cricket ground out through the gate in the fence at the bottom of the garden.

I think that was one of the few times that we got a serious hiding, not from Dad, but from Mum. She was more than a bit brassed off about her precious antique oak tray to say the least! That's when the "Marble Holocaust" began.

To this day I think we had an informer in our midst. It must have been a girl! Normally informers were, but I was the "blamee" most of the time. Sean had hidden the tray behind the old gramophone in the linen cupboard and there was no way Mum could have found it without help in a hundred years.

Finding anything in the shambles within the walls of 29 Poole Street took ages at the best of times. Even when the home was sold, in 1982 after Mum and Dad had passed away, items re-surfaced that had been misplaced since 1951!

One of these items was a final term school report from my last year at the convent school. It was in the inside pocket of one of Dad's old suits. A note was pinned to it addressed to Dad from Sister Gabriel, asking why my school attendance record for the period was "dismal to say the least". Dad was requested to "please explain" and could he attend a meeting with her in the very near future to discuss the matter. I know he never made the meeting. I also know that he did not want to tell her that my absence was caused by an exceptionally good whitebait season!

Nurse Vondersmidt

She had to be about twenty-five years old, short, honey blond and a little on the plump side but not fat. Her "shortness" probably made her look "fattish" but she probably wasn't to grownups. She also had green eyes. I don't know for sure where she lived. I think it may have been in an old house behind the picture theatre, which had been converted into a boarding house for teachers. If she had a boyfriend, I sure hope he had false teeth. If not, he soon would have as she sure needed the practice. Outside of school, no one ever seemed to talk about her or even see her in the town.

I reckon she was German but she had no accent. Probably didn't tell anyone if she was a kraut because it was only nine years since the war ended. To many people Germans were still a bit on the outer, so to speak. Sort of like divorcées during those days. There was quite a stigma to it if you were a kraut or a divorcee. Then again, she could have been Austrian,

Dutch or even Swedish and if so, then I owe her an apology.

To my knowledge, there was only one divorcée in the town and although I didn't realise it at the time, it must have been very difficult for her to bring up her four kids. There was no such thing as maintenance payments. The family benefit that everyone got was all there was. Mum was forever giving the divorcée second and third hand clothes and bits and pieces for her kids.

Anyway, Nurse Vondersmidt was not exactly most kids' best friend. Nor would she ever be voted the most popular member of Parklands School's staff by the kids for obvious reasons – she was the dental nurse!

The worst part of the journey home from school was the circumnavigation of the dental surgery. It was a relief and feeling of joy just to sneak past the dental nurse's little weatherboard hut without her nabbing you for a quick check up. To a five year old the "clovish" smell alone that emanated from the surgery was enough to make you vomit. Inside was the little torture maid. Visits were compulsory when you got the little white card to attend and no excuses were acceptable. The nurse grabbed you and sat you up on the stuffed leather chair surrounded by all her instruments of torture.

Even to this day, especially when I sit in a dentist's chair, I can still picture her. A red armband with a swastika on it and gold and red "SS" pins in the tips of her blouse collars. I must have imagined her wearing them at the time. Confusing her with a kraut in the war comics we used to buy or "borrow" from Buddens' Bookshop.

There were no X-rays and she used the blunt end of a steel dental instrument to tap the end of each tooth quite ruthlessly. If one of the taps made you jump or bite her hand then that would be the tooth she would aim to attack. No injections were ever given and she would dive into your mouth to find a spot on the tooth in which to drill a hole or two.

The drilling was done with a foot peddle operated machine or "buzzer" as we called it. Quite similar to Mum's old Singer sewing machine except that it had a long pivotal arm that swung out over your head. The drill was attached to the end of the arm. You would be sitting there in absolute fear, gripping the sides of the chair. Knuckles white. Ten little indentations immediately became cast into the armrests.

The nurse's left hand would be jammed into your mouth to keep it open and many a time she gave me a slap around the ears for biting her. Once she had dug the hole in the tooth, she jammed what tasted like a hundred pure cloves into it and pity help you if you tried to spit them out.

Then she sat there on her swivel stool singing what seemed to me, the German national anthem, while mixing up the mercury and stuff she was going to jam into the hole she had dug. You were in the chair, tears streaming down your cheeks. She would rummage around in a drawer and come out with a thin flat piece of stainless steel about two inches long. She would wind it around her fountain pen into a circle and then force it down between the perfectly innocent tooth and its mates. Right down to the gums. Obviously, she didn't know how much that hurt. On the other hand, maybe she did! She'd then grab a ratchet type gadget, attach the steel band to it, and screw it up tight, supposedly so the tooth could not escape. I don't know because at those times I could not talk to ask the questions. She finally rammed the concoction she had mixed up consisting mainly of pure mercury, lead and the equivalent in those days of liquid nails, into the hole in your tooth. She did this with what seemed like a nail punch and a hammer. It was hard to tell because your eyes would be more than tightly closed.

With gums bleeding and the odd hole in your tongue where she had intentionally jammed the buzzer to warn you to keep your mouth open and keep still, you slid off the chair. Your pants would be wet with sweat and as you stood you would have to pull the back seam of them and your undies from your bum. Even if air conditioning was invented then, it would take another thirty years to find its way to Motueka.

Nurse Vondersmidt then pulled out a little white box with an inkpad in it, then a rubber stamp with a pussycat on it and another little box of stick-on stars. The stamps were imprinted on the back of other kids' hands.

She never gave me either but just taunted me with them saying that all the other kids got them for being good while she monstered their mouths. She said that I would "never ever" get a pussycat or a star if I kept behaving the way I did.

I "never ever" wanted a pussycat on my hand or one of her bloody stars in fact I told her on many occasions that I was "never ever" coming back. She replied that she would come and find me wherever I was hiding. Just like the Nazis rounding up the Jews I thought. To this day, my teeth are completely buggered thanks to that witch.

Goldilocks

My younger sister Veronica had the most beautiful long, thick blond hair. She would spend hours washing, grooming, sun drying, combing and brushing it and sometimes Mum would plait it. One Saturday morning Veronica had spent hours performing this task. She then sat in the kitchen secretly hoping that everyone who walked past would comment on how beautiful her hair looked.

Sean had had enough of this preening. As he walked past her, he lifted his leg in an exaggerated fashion and ripped a huge noisy fart directly at "Ronk's" hair. He was barely six inches away from her golden locks. Ronk burst into tears. Mum shrieked with rage and disgust. Sean bolted, and Kerry, Francie and I burst out laughing making sure we were not within Mum's striking distance. Mum took off to the bathroom with a sobbing Veronica to re-wash, comb, sun dry and brush her hair all over again.

What Mum and Veronica did not know was that Sean's trick was only pretence and the fart was a manufactured one. The art of doing so was to cup your hand under your armpit. When you levered your arm downwards, the compression between the cupped hand and the armpit made the same sound. The extra hair wash was all in vain.

Ironically, years later, Sean wore his hair in long golden locks, halfway down his back. I for one, would never have even contemplated farting on it for he was then at the height of his boxing career.

Night Riders,
The "Little Blue Coupe"
and Gladdy Brougham

I can't remember the make or model of the car. It may have been a Pontiac. It looked like the one Noddy and Big Ears roamed around in but it was Americanised. It had one of those boots that opened out from the top and when open, two or three kids could sit there. It was probably built in about 1930 and only had two doors, a single front bench seat and was painted blue, hence its nickname, "The Little Blue Coupe". If that wasn't enough to distinguish it, there was a hole through the rear window where Kerry had slogged a cricket ball. I remember the hit, a great shot down to the long-on boundary over the garage. Unfortunately, his aim was just a fraction low but he probably had his eyes closed at the time.

From time to time and for months at a time, Dad used to look after the LBC for a mate of his called Peter Tahau, who used to go off on trips to the North Island. Peter was quite distinguishable as well. He had three fingers blown off his right hand and he reckoned that happened in the Second World War. He seemed so old to us that it probably really happened in the Maori Wars! Lopped off by a spear or something similar, I reckoned.

My oldest brother and sister, Pat and Hilary, were at high school and probably fourteen and fifteen years old, so I would have been about five years old. Dad used to park the LBC in the driveway after work. He would then mess about in the garden or go fishing for an hour or so, have tea and then bugger off, either walking or biking to his second job at the local picture theatre.

Some nights Mum would be out at a flower show or horticulture meeting and when this happened Pat and Hilary would decide it was time for a spin in the LBC. Sean, Kerry and I would be pretending to be asleep, and at Pat's signal, a tap on the wall, Sean and I would jump out the bedroom window and help push the LBC in reverse down the driveway. We had to do this in the dark so that Mr Crisp next door would not see or hear us and so that the tyre marks in the grass driveway would not be so noticeable.

Kerry would stay at home to babysit Veronica and Francie. That was his job because he really did not bloom into these sorts of shenanigans until during and after his stint in the seminary. Then he really made up for lost time. However, those are his stories to tell.

Pat, Hilary, Sean and I would push the LBC down the street with its lights off until it was doing about ten miles an hour. Then Pat would jump in, whack it in gear and drop the clutch. It would fire up, he would stop, we would all pile in, and we would be off on a joyride around the back streets of the town still in our pyjamas, with the car lights off. It was quite hair raising at the time. Even when I think of it nowadays, it sends a bit of a shudder up my spine. Simply the dire consequences if we ever had a prang, if we were caught by the local cop, or if Dad came home early from the picture theatre, which happened from time to time but never during an LBC night excursion.

Many years later, I found out why I was allowed to go on these joyrides.

I was always teased about being Dad's boy and Pat, Hilary and Sean knew that I would dob them in if they didn't take me with them.

While on the topic of Dad's second job at the picture theatre, the theatre also had an ice-cream shop attached. A woman called Gladdy Brougham owned it. The shop had high serving counters. A five or six year old had to reach up to counter height and blindly grope around for any stray chocolate bars or boxes of Jaffas, chocolate-coated peanuts and raisins or Minties. Sometimes the odd chocolate fish or teddy bear got in your hand's way. The chocolate bars were either the one shilling and threepence size or the two shillings and sixpence size. The chocolate frogs and fish were threepence.

Plundering Gladdy Brougham's could be quite hazardous. All she could see was a little hand sneaking up over the counter groping for anything within range. Often the hand would be grabbed by Gladdy from the other side. She could do nothing but hang on for dear life because of the big ice-cream freezers on her side of the counter. They were waist high for an adult and three feet from front to back. There was no way for her to see whose hand she had hold of. I remember getting out of a "hand clamp" on a couple of occasions by swinging by the arm Gladdy had in her vice-like grip, with my feet off the floor. When the weight got too much for her she had to let go. I'd fall to the floor and scramble on my hands and knees either out of the front door of the shop or out through the adjoining door into the foyer of the theatre. Here, Mr Lark the owner, had placed huge bunches of red velvet curtains in various positions such as in corners. It was easy for small people to hide behind them. Out the front door was the fastest escape route. Not only that, Gladdy had to run around the counter, open a latch and then go after you. It rather slowed her down a bit. She would never leave the front door of the shop however for she knew that a brother or mate might be waiting at the door of the theatre, ready to rip in and clean her out in her absence!

Gladdy gazumped us in the end however. She put these bloody great mirrors on the opposite wall to the counter. Almost a violation of human rights at the time I thought. Just like video cameras in the workplace today. We did not know that we had been sprung until Dad came home from the picture theatre one night without our usual treat of a chocolate fish. He probably pinched them as well. Just kidding! He came into the bedroom and said we had had enough chocolate "on the house" from Gladdy's and told us about the mirrors. Something our intelligence people had missed. Gladdy had obviously had a little "chat" with Dad.

Dad also reckoned that Gladdy's takings doubled after that and that's when she sold out to Mr Hartshorne. In hindsight I am not proud of the hammering we gave her ice cream shop. She was a nice old bird. Sorry Gladdy.

As kids, we saw many movies at that theatre. Mostly black and white westerns preceded by the news with two kookaburras as the intro. One had a flea on its breast and the other had a tiny feather on the end of its beak! The last movie I saw there was "Sink the Bismarck". My greatest memory of the theatre however, was seeing a live performance of the Everly Brothers. Yes, Don and Phil Everly on stage at the piss pot little Motueka picture theatre. Live, they sounded just like their records and it was a great performance. I guess today, a similar performance in Motueka would be the equivalent of The Rolling Stones doing a live performance at Strachan in Tasmania.

The Famous Fan Palm Tree

I had never seen a fire brigade in action until the day the famous fan palm tree burned down.

I had seen the displays and competitions they used to hold out in the park, which was accessible through the back garden gate. These were fire-fighting competitions, between the local townships' fire brigades. The fire fighters would all line up and use the hoses as water cannons, aiming at flat bits of steel hinged to the tops of poles. The objective was to shoot the steel plates over to prove how accurate the fire fighters were, I thought. I could never figure this out, as I had never seen a house with a pole sticking up on it and a flat bit of metal on the pole. Perhaps I had missed something here.

I also could not figure out why they had to have these competitions at all. Who really cared who could put a fire out the fastest, if this was the object of the exercise. Not only that, Mum used to give these blokes a rev up every time they practised in the park. She would walk out and tell them to stop wasting water and that if they wanted to do something useful, then they should come and water her garden. Dad asked her not to rev them up in case we ever had a real fire for they may not come. Perhaps he had a premonition!

If the best fire fighting brigade in the district was in a town 100 miles away did that mean that if we had a fire in our town we would have to wait until the best and fastest fire fighters got there? I don't think so, and I rested my case. Mum was right again, practising shooting at metal plates on poles really was a waste of water.

Although our house stood on a large block of land, the front lawn was quite small and all sorts of shrubs and trees surrounded it. In the middle of the lawn was a fan palm tree. These palms have a trunk covered with many layers of woven or thatched hair-like material left from previous growth. As the tree grows the thatch stays behind, the palms drop off, and new palm leaves, or fans, sprout.

At the very top of the tree, at any given time of the year, there would be approximately twenty of the live green palm fronds. They were shaped like a large version of a fan one would use to produce cool air when waved in front of your face for a cooling effect. The tree itself is of no practical use and more ornamental than anything else.

Our fan palm was about fifty feet high and probably about a hundred years old. The fact that it was the only specimen of its type for miles around made it a bit of a local attraction. Gardening friends of Mum's would come from "all over the show" to admire the famous Poole Street fan palm tree. Mum thought it was a pretty good specimen. She reckoned it complemented her other plants and trees such as her fragrantissimum bush, the red Japanese maple, the sycamore, the blue hydrangeas and the native rimu tree, all dotted around the garden.

To us and probably to Dad it was just another tree, one of many in our gardens. "The more trees, the less lawn to mow," he'd say. He would rather be fishing or at the pub than mowing lawns.

My brother Kerry was a great fan of matches, regardless of whether it was close to Guy Fawkes Day or not. Late one afternoon he and Sean, another brother, were busy lighting little fires around the place. They decided to drop a match at the base of the famous Poole Street fan palm tree. The resulting fire was an unbelievable sight!

The fan palm was only about fifteen feet from the front of the house and it seemed that the flames shot up the tree at a million miles an hour. It was a spectacular sight in the late evening as flames spewed high into the air. Sparks and smoke were whipped away by the breeze, across the roofs of the other old timber weather boarded houses down the street. Red-hot ashes flew through the air like millions of fireflies. All the houses in the whole bloody street downwind of us could have gone up in smoke but they didn't. Now that would have been something to write about!

Anyway, now we had a real fire engine and a real fire outside our house. In spite of the fact that we didn't have a metal plate on a pole on our house, or on the famous fan palm tree, the firemen took three times as long to get their hoses going as they took in practice in the park. Dad was getting a bit anxious. Probably making plans for the future in bolting a couple of poles on the roof with metal plates on. Presumably to help the fire fighters with their accuracy and timing as a "just in case" measure.

Eventually the fire fighters got their act together. "Perhaps they are just stalling for time, waiting for the audience to get bigger," yelled Sean to Kerry who was hiding under the canopy of the red Japanese maple bush. He was trying to dig a hole to bury the box of matches.

Heaps of people gathered to watch the event and even a police officer was there turning back cars that wanted to drive past. The cop had arrived on his pushbike, standard police issue in those days, as there was no police car in the town.

People had followed the sirens and all the neighbours from several streets around had now gathered in the street. Mr Steer, ever alert, watchful and helpful, was there with a bucket, boom and ladder, his one-man fire-fighting kit. I think he kept a complete emergency kit just inside the front door of his house, which was diagonally over the road from us, just for emergencies at the Horgans'. Like the time he rescued me from sixty feet up in the walnut tree, in a howling gale, with Sean on the ground below yelling for me to jump! Sean had enticed me up there in the first place.

Meanwhile, back at the fire, we had everything going at once. Two fire trucks, an audience of hundreds, cops, and even an ambulance was rumoured to be on its way from Nelson, a city some thirty miles away. "What a ripping afternoon," yelled Kerry as he sneaked out the front gate and into the sanctuary of Crisp's house next door.

The tree seemed to burn for ages. As the layered hairy thatch on the trunk burned, wave after wave of rings of fire zoomed up the tree. The crowd cheered each wave. Eventually, however, the practice in the park paid off for the fire fighters as they zeroed in, and the "fire lighters" regrouped and sat forlorn in a large puddle on the grass.

All that was left of the "Famous Fan Palm Tree" was a sodden black stump in the front lawn. The lawn itself looked like one we were used to after a long hot summer, all brown and cracked, except it was now under water. At least Mum got one of her wishes that evening. The fire brigade watered her garden!

Windows in the front rooms had cracked from the heat of the flames. Dad had lots of practice at replacing windows so that wouldn't be too much of a problem. The red paint on the roof and the green and cream paint on the front wall of the house was now blistered brown.

Mum was standing in the front garden trying desperately to stake up some of the many plants that had been mowed down by the fire fighters and their hoses. Tears were streaming down her cheeks at the thought of the loss of the fan palm. At the same time, she was threatening the fire fighters with a broom if they dared do any more damage to her garden. Our house and all the others in the street could have burned down for all she cared. Her garden had always come first, but not this day!

Dad, by this time, resigned to this sort of prank, from three little boys whose heritage he must have often questioned, sat on the singed front verandah. He silently took out his "makings", rolled and smoked a cigarette, probably wishing he were at the pub. He would be later, along with his mates in the volunteer fire brigade, laughing the whole episode off. I am sure there were times that Dad secretly enjoyed some of our antics and was proud of our inventiveness.

Like the Famous Fan Palm Tree, Mum went into her equally famous mute mode. This time for a week, and Dad had a bit of a win here.

The enquiry was yet to come!

Dad "had his suspicions" as to who the culprit was and he knew very well that the blame would be dumped squarely on me! I got the blame for all of the pranks simply because I was the youngest and the so-called Dad's boy. In the end, if I remember, no concrete evidence was ever found as to who lit the match but I overheard Dad tell Mum, "I've got it narrowed down to three small suspects".

The grit could really have hit the fan, so to speak, over this stunt we three thought, but there was no fan left for the grit to hit.

The Window

Uncle Allan married Dad's sister, Auntie Roie. They had a three thousand acre farm eighteen miles up the Motueka River from the township of Motueka. They grew tobacco, farmed sheep, had a few cows, the odd horse, and in later years sold the property to a forestry concern. They moved to Christchurch and retired to play golf.

Uncle Allan was a good cricketer and played a mean round of golf as well. Two of his sons would also shine in later years in both rugby and cricket. The oldest son, "Young Allan," could well have been an All Black, but his love of cars got in the way a bit. He had an uncanny knack of regularly writing them off!

In those days, golf was considered more of a sport for gentlemen. It was expensive to buy golf clubs and pay membership fees. Aside from that, as kids, we had more important things with which to occupy our time.

I pinched an old golf ball from the boot of Uncle Allan's car one Sunday when they came to visit. It bounced high on the concrete and that is about all we could do with it, as a golf club was way out of our reach. I suppose I could have pinched a golf club from the boot of his car as well but I didn't think of it at the time and Uncle Allan would have been a bit pissed off if I had.

My brother Sean however decided that he could make a golf club. The shaft was a manuka tomato stake and the head was from one of Dad's old hammers. The grip was green twine bound around the upper end of the stake. The hammerhead was jammed onto the end of the stake and a couple of nails were hammered into the end of the stake to wedge the hammerhead in place. "Perfect," he reckoned.

The next day, Monday, was a beautiful summer's morning. It was seven o'clock and as usual, the three of us, Sean, Kerry and I were up and ready for school. We had a couple of hours to kill. I was five, Kerry six, and Sean was seven years old.

Our home sat on the front of a quarter acre block; the front door faced the road. If you walked through the front entrance and kept walking down the wide hallway, you would end up in the bathroom, in front of the hand basin. Above the basin was a mirror on the wall. To the right of the hand basin and mirror and in the same wall, was a three-foot high by two-foot wide opaque window. If you could have seen through it, which you could not, you would see the clothesline, some twenty yards in front of you. The clothesline was in the centre of the grassed back yard.

Backtracking, upon entering the front door and walking a pace or two down the hallway, off to the left was Mum and Dad's bedroom. Opposite, on the right was the door to the lounge or sitting room. The sitting room had an open fireplace and a mantelpiece above it. On the mantelpiece there was a gap where an family heirloom chiming clock used to sit. It was away at the jewellers being repaired. Kerry had previously seen to its demise.

Another door led out of the sitting room to the bedroom my sisters had commandeered. Down the main hallway on the left, a door led into our oldest brother Pat's bedroom. Further down, was the door into a very large bedroom which belonged to Sean, Kerry and me. Slightly opposite our bedroom, on the right hand side of the hallway was another door. This led into the dining room, then to the kitchen and then out to the enclosed back porch.

Off the porch, doors led into the dunny and to the laundry or washhouse. Dad had added these two rooms a year or two before. Prior to that, the dunny was a single seater short drop, down in the garden.

If you walked out the back door, turned hard left and walked about seven paces, you would be directly outside the opaque bathroom window. If you were back inside the bathroom standing at the hand basin, you could look into the mirror, used over the years for Dad's 7 a.m. shave. Sean also used it for hair combing and pimple squeezing in his last years at high school.

This beautiful Monday morning seemed just perfect for the christening of the new golf club. The tee was a matchbox outer and Kerry placed the golf ball on it while Sean took a few practice swings. He had seen Arnold Palmer do this in the sports section of the shorts before the main matinee at the pictures on Saturday afternoon. Kerry and I did not know what the hell he was talking about and sure as hell did not know who Arnold Palmer was. We doubted there even was such a bloke, especially with a strange name like that. I was fortunate enough to meet this Arnold Palmer some years later, in America.

Anyway, Sean was to be the first to have a whack at the ball because he was the oldest and the club was his idea, even though I was the one who pinched the golf ball! I was to be last ... naturally.

The rotary clothesline, as mentioned earlier, was twenty yards from the house on the back lawn. The general direction of the intended hit zone was the back of the house, to the right of the opaque bathroom window. This was a large area of weatherboard with no windows, and the rear wall of our bedroom.

The only blemishes on this wall were about a million red cricket ball marks and about the same number of dirt coloured tennis ball kisses. The red marks were best described as "dents". These were made when the keeper, usually me, dodged an angry throw due to a dropped prior catch or stumping miss, or by balls snicked past slips for four runs. There were dozens of tennis and cricket balls under the house that had made their way there via the smashed-in mesh vents at ground level in the weatherboards. The stumps of the house were too low for us to crawl under to retrieve the balls.

The hit zone had to be towards the house for two reasons: One, we only had one golf ball and the house would stop it so that we could all get a hit. Two, if the hit zone was in the opposite direction, a huge plum tree was in the way.

Sean stepped to the tee. He took an almighty swing with the club, which was as long as he was tall, and missed the ball by at least two feet. Reluctantly he handed the club to Kerry and because Kerry and I were a lot shorter than Sean, we stood on a wooden apple box. Kerry's swing was woeful and because he had not been allowed a practice swing, he claimed another.

Neither Sean nor Kerry would go on to take up the sport of golf I thought, and in hindsight I was right. Kerry's second swing was even worse than the first. The hammerhead hit the ground and the club bounced up giving the ball a tiny nudge. It wobbled and fell off the matchbox while the club continued upwards and tangled in the wires of the clothes line. By standing on the apple box, now on its end, I had the task to untangle the club or I would not get a shot. Once I had done that, it was finally my turn. Yes!

Sean and Kerry obviously figured they would get another shot simply because if they couldn't hit the ball then nor could I. Anyway, if they didn't let me have a hit, then I would tell Dad, "Cos I was the youngest" and I was Dad's boy.

I climbed up on the apple box and ripped in with a big looping swing.

Yes again. It was howling through the air. It was all kind of like slow motion. I had looked down at the ball, as you are supposed to, said Arnold Palmer via Sean. But lo and behold when I opened my eyes, the ball was still sitting on the matchbox.

At this stage, our eyes became riveted on the opaque bathroom window towards which a hammerhead was hurtling, at like nine hundred miles an hour! It must have come loose when Kerry belted it into the ground. End over end it went, and it was precisely "shave time!"

Exclamations of horror and shock. The use of words such as the "F" word were not known to us at that stage, and shit, or J.... C...... were never used, but the word "run" was simultaneously uttered. This was obviously the most practical and appropriate word to use at the time.

We could not get out of the blocks fast enough. The ex-Canterbury sprint champion was hopefully standing in front of the mirror, just to the left of the window.

We were still glued to the spot, waiting to see the carnage as the window exploded. It seemed to take forever, but it was in reality about a second. Then it hit! It was like a shotgun blast through a shop front window in the movies. Then came the scream of the old man seemingly having a heart attack. His face peered through the gaping hole in the window. A face half covered in shaving cream and half shaved. Slow motion gave way to real time and we were off, heading down the garden path, three abreast on a path built for two.

We got to the plum tree as Dad managed to rip down the hallway, hook a left through the dining room, another left through the kitchen, then left out the back door. Finally a right onto the path and now he had a straight run at us.

We had a forty-yard start on him and had another thirty to go before we made the gate out into the park. At that point, our usual trick was to split up. The old man or Mum, whoever was the chaser at the time, got confused as to which of us to go after, and gave up the chase. Not this morning!

We didn't think he would dare run out into the park in his pyjamas. He didn't have to. I had once heard Mum say that he was quick, but not that quick. He got us, a yard before the gate. He had us now. Kerry and I were squirming under one arm and Sean was under the other, all screaming for our lives to be spared. The old man marched up the path back towards the house. Sean and Kerry stopped screaming and started to lay all the blame on me because it happened on my turn. Bastards! Same old trick.

Mum had been watching the whole thing from the window over the kitchen sink, her normal place. Neither Dad nor any of us boys knew how to work the sink and never would while we were at 29 Poole Street. She walked outside with her trademark pursed lips and waited on the back step for the outcome. Hole in one I would have thought!

As Dad passed the clothesline, he kicked the wooden apple box across the lawn where it came to rest against the house, beneath the broken bathroom window. He plonked us all down on the box to "serve sentence." "At exactly half past five this evening you three will be seated on this box, is that clear?"

"Yes," to the power of three was the answer. He would be a bit pissed off today because he could not stop off at the Post Office pub for a beer on the way home. I saw a bit of a grin on Mum's face when he said this, because she was forever having a shot at him for his daily pub stop.

At five thirty that afternoon, we waited seated on the apple box under the broken bathroom window, staring at the back gate for Dad's grand entrance. He came striding through the gate, whistling a tune and carrying a new pane of glass under his arm. While wrapped in brown paper, we knew exactly what it was.

He marched down the path, between the vegetable garden and the gladioli beds, under the plum tree, past the clothesline and then headed straight for us. "You're in for it now Nick," whispered Sean.

"The sentence is the lesson, and you had better pay attention and be mighty civil." That is all Dad said. "Mighty civil" was another of his phrases when addressing us en masse. We paid attention and were mighty civil. I learned a lot that day. The lesson was how to install a new window. The "glazier" had a part time job as the assistant postmaster! Dad must have left work early to get the glass from Mr Smith, the glass man. We would get to know Mr Smith pretty well over the next six or seven years.

We were in awe as the lesson began. "He must have broken a few windows as well when he was young to be able to do this," whispered Kerry.

It is a pity window installation changed dramatically a few years later. The introduction of alloy frames and rubber beading, as opposed to putty, wooden mouldings and pin tacks would take all the fun out of it. The three of us could have been experts in that field if we had have taken up glazing as a trade.

First Dad chipped out all the old dried putty and removed all the broken shards of glass. Then he carefully wrapped the glass pieces in the brown paper that came with the new glass, and placed it in the rubbish bin. Next was the removal of the tiny pins and the wooden beading strips. He kept the pins and the beading for re-use. Waste not, want not, I guess.

He scraped away all the old paint, putty and dust, sanded the cutaway where the new glass was to be seated and gave it a coat of primer. He explained the whole process, every tiny detail that is, adding that if you replace a rotted window frame, remember to put the glass back the same way it was before. That meant the side that faced the outside should be replaced facing the outside. He reckoned that the wind and elements would bend glass inwards over time. If you reverse old glass, then the slightest wind pressure in the future will break it. "Mind boggling," whispered Sean.

Even Mum had joined us and was watching, seeming to take it all in. I noted that Dad eyed her from time to time, silently asking why she bothered as her job was in the kitchen, in the laundry, cooking and looking after kids. He was strange like that but never said it aloud.
He had a small carton of putty and linseed oil. He worked both substances

into a chewing gum like consistency. A thin layer of putty was layered in the vertical and horizontal recess all around the window frame. When the new glass was positioned into the frame's recesses, he ever so lightly pressed it against the soft new putty. The wooden beading was then replaced and the small nails were tacked in place. Three nails on each edge of the glass to act as a further aid to stop the glass from falling out of the recess. Dad was careful not to let the nails touch the glass but have them sit a fraction of an inch out from it. A rim of putty was then placed completely around the outer edge of the glass.

Now for the finishing touches. First with his thumb he smoothed the putty against the glass and the edge of the window recess. With the putty knife he bevelled the putty so that it would let any water run off the glass and frame. This also gave the glazing job a "professional look". Once finished, he took a rag moistened with turpentine and cleaned the window of any putty smears.

At last, he stood back a few feet from the window to admire his handiwork and perhaps get a cheer from the apprentices. Almost like Michaelangelo studying his work on the ceiling of the Sistine Chapel. All three of us, and Mum, reckoned he should get a medal for this performance. He had a broad smile on his face as he admired his job. Suddenly, the smile changed to a slight frown as he noticed an ever so slight indent. There was a thumbprint in the putty in the bottom left hand corner of the window.

He walked to the window, peered intently at the thumbprint, and smoothed it out with the turpentine-impregnated rag wrapped over his finger. He stood back a bit and then as a final touch, deftly used the putty knife to re-define the bevel.

"Hells bells!" he yelped as he jumped back in horror. We saw it the split second he heard it. A crack started to move across the corner of the glass from the exact spot where he had made his final little re-adjustment. It was slowly heading in a forty-five degree direction up and across the glass. For some unexplained reason the crack slowed and stopped about twelve inches into its journey.

The old man very rarely swore. "I'll be damned," he said. "Bugger! Bugger! Bugger!" he said in a loud voice that ripped across the neighbourhood. This time we three bolted to a safe distance to hide behind Mum. She was not very tall, but after seven kids, was pretty wide.

This was not our doing. He had his chance earlier in the day to give us a belting and now this new break was his fault and his problem, we thought. He knew it too but there was no way he was going to let it get the better of him. He would win out in the end, come hell or high water.

Dad stormed off towards the shed. We heard angry sawing and banging and then he returned with two small pieces of plywood, each about six inches by three inches. He drilled quarter inch holes at each end of the crack in the glass. These holes corresponded with pre-drilled holes in the pieces of plywood. He had two small bolts, nuts and washers. He intended to place a piece of plywood on both sides of the window and use the bolts to tie it together, sort of like a sandwich. There were no electric drills in those days and he performed the operation with a hand drill. No mean feat we thought, drilling through glass that is!

We three had now gathered closer as his demeanour had returned almost to normal and we felt safe that a belting was not likely. Actually, the old man never ever laid a hand on any of us. He promised to and threatened us with the odd hiding but never got around to it. He did cuff our sisters once and a while but being girls, they always deserved it!

With Mum's help from the inside of the window, Dad gently placed the plywood pieces, slid in the bolts, slipped on the washers and gingerly tightened the nuts. He did not trust us to help we thought collectively. The smile returned to his face and although Michaelangelo's window on the Sistine Chapel's ceiling now looked like an angel with three wings, he didn't seem to care. He was simply resolved not to buy another pane of glass. Mr Smith would think he was a dummy, and Dad knew that before long we would probably break the window again anyway.

He knew his boys had scarcely embarked on their reign of terror and mayhem, when it came to breaking windows. He was right but would be proved wrong on that particular window! What amazed me was how this window managed to survive another ten years of backyard blitz, cricket, golf, football and general goofing off while we kids were still at home.

Dad passed away in 1978 and Mum in 1982. They were both just sixty-four years old. In the days immediately after Mum's funeral, we were readying the house for sale. I happened to glance at the bathroom window. Not a mark on it except for two small pieces of plywood bolted through the glass. They had lasted twenty-seven years! I often wondered what the new owners thought of those two bits of plywood.

In 2003, I drove past the old house on one of my infrequent trips to Motueka. I stopped outside the house. The owner, who was in the front garden, quite rightly asked if there was something or someone I was looking for. I explained that I was raised in that house and that it held fond memories. He invited me in and as I walked around the back of the house, I noted that the ply on the window was still in place and yet the whole house had been completely renovated.

I never asked why the glass had not been changed and never told the owner that the plywood patch had been on the window for forty-eight years. Not only that, I didn't have a spare day to tell him the story behind it.

Early in 2008, I returned to the house once more to get some photos for this book and noticed that the window had finally been replaced. In the back yard, there were two small boys, a cricket bat and a football or two. I had the answer.

The Footy Team

I believe that a prerequisite to starting up a private school, Catholic or otherwise, was that you had to have a minimum of forty or so odd kids. "Odd" being a reasonable choice of word. The percentage of Catholic kids in a town with a population of barely 3,000 was not that great. Therefore, the Catholic hierarchy scoured the countryside for anyone remotely linked to Catholicism. They were still short of about three kids but somehow they managed to find three dubious or "renegade" families within the town. They must have threatened them with hell when they died and so the sons of the renegades showed up for school.

These three kids were then thirteen or fourteen years old and huge. They should have been at secondary school. They were the sort of blokes who would, as soon as they possibly could, lie their way out of school altogether. They were destined for the work force where they would surely make their mark.

All three of these blokes Kevin, Anthony and John, were street wise already and they became an asset to the school in many ways. They were the protectors of the little kids against the marauding Protestants of the two state schools in the town. The Catholic school was located in between the two state schools and the Catholic kids often had to walk the gauntlet to and from school. Kevin, Anthony and John lived at intervals down the main street, in sort of safe houses along the way. These three were "close to heathens", as the nuns would say. To me, as a six year old, they were close to giants. They were sort of like "Gullivers" from the fairy tale, and the rest of us were the Lilliputians.

Statistically speaking, there were about twenty two and a half boys and twenty two and a half girls at the Catholic primary school and to get a fifteen-boy rugby team together was a bit of a trick. First, you had to weed out the sissies and the ones who wanted to play hockey (such as my brother Sean), which was much the same thing. This left us with seventeen boys, fifteen on the run on team, one reserve and one ball boy. This could be Sean or a girl if things got tight.

Of the seventeen, there were two Horgans, four Roborghs, three Stebbings, a Small, a Westbury, a Strong, a couple of Stephens and the three Gullivers. Two of the Gullivers made up the front row with our smallest player, the hooker, hanging between them. Phillip Stephens was our hooker. He was about three feet tall, three feet wide, had no neck and he hung a good two feet off the ground between the two front row props. He'd be swinging around somewhere within the scrum, his feet groping about searching for the ball while the two "Gullivers" either side of him would be engaging in a bit of innocent eye gouging, head butting, biting and the likes!

The referee was normally the recently arrived parish priest. He also refereed the local senior competition. He often ignored the goings on in the scrums probably because he was our coach as well! The third Gulliver was the fullback. The Gullivers were not much good at playing rugby. Well they were, but because they were so big, I think they did not want to hurt the little kids and so they just played along and looked menacing. Boy did they scare the crap out of our competitors. We also had a hell of a weight advantage in the scrums.

The nuns decreed that we had to have a rugby uniform and so they decided that we needed to do a "bob a job" campaign in the town. This was also going to be a trick because most of the houses we had to approach were full of Protestants whose kids went to the State schools. Why would they support such a scheme for the Catholic school? The target was twenty-two pounds, which was a hell of a lot of money in those days for sixteen football jerseys. At a bob a job that would be a staggering four hundred and forty jobs. Somehow, we managed it but some of us made up our own rules and approached the houses and their owners mentioning that the job and bob parts of the "bob a job" were optional. Two bob was a bit more reasonable I thought, and often the job part of it was substituted for "donation!"

I remember Reggie Collins, who had just built a new house, really taking me up on the job part. He offered me a bob to cart and stack two bloody great cords of firewood he had just had delivered. I remember trying to decline the bob, and the job, but there was no way out. I started on the first barrow load and it took me until dark. Reggie had to go to football practice and I bolted as soon as he left. I had made sure that he had given me the bob in advance though. I never returned!

I ran into Reggie forty years later. I was hoping he had forgotten the "bob" I had pinged him for when I was seven years old. He never mentioned it.

It is my understanding that the kids at St Peter Chanel's Catholic primary school still use that same set of rugby jerseys some fifty years later. Must have had a bunch of sissies playing football there since our day! I hope Simon Mannering, the current New Zealand rugby league representative and ex convent school old boy, doesn't read this.

All the other schools in the area had lots more kids. The two town State schools had 600 and 250 kids respectively and yet more often than not we would beat them. My brother Kerry, Robert Roborgh and Michael Small were our super stars. The other schools had their stars as well, but not three in any given team. Our fullback, Anthony "Gulliver" also helped make us quite a formidable unit.

In my last year at the convent primary school, I captained the team although there were two other players who would probably have done the job better. They were Michael Small and Rudy Roborgh. In my second year at high school I was selected to play in the first fifteen. This was quite rare for a fourteen year old in form four. In fact in my final year at high school, after a stint away at boarding school, on occasions, I was fortunate enough to captain that side.

It is quite interesting looking back at those teams from the local and district schools. Some individual stars in each school stood out and went on to represent their province, some even New Zealand as All Blacks in later years. I name some of them here as I was always impressed with the way they played and in particular, the spirit in which they played. Darryl Fry from Riwaka, Allan Thorn from Dovedale, Bill Lucre from Brooklyn, Terry Mitchell from Takaka, Johnny Bowers and Wayne Eagers from Parklands and Steve Scott from Motueka South, to name just a few from our era.

It's funny how I often thought that given that the main primary school was called Parklands, and our school was St Peter Chanel, the Education Department could have surely come up with a better name than "Motueka South School". Probably named after the common criminal element that came from the southern end of the town!

One Sunday morning the great Bob Scott, an All Black of *immortal* fame, gave a goal kicking display at the local rugby ground. I was about six years old at the time and after mass or church that morning, half the town turned out for the event. Bob had either retired from the sport or was about to. He was in Motueka to play for a team called the Buccaneers, made up from promising young players, has-beens and wannabes but would neverbes.

Bob Scott must have been really old because I remember that he was almost bald! What made a greater impression, in spite of the baldness, was that he was bare footed this particular morning. He placed the football on the halfway line and kicked it cleanly between the goal posts, not once but three times in succession. He only had three kicks and got the lot over. What was even more spectacular was that unlike modern day goal kickers, he placed the ball in a divot mark in the grass he had previously made with his heel, took exactly six steps directly backwards, paused, ran in and kicked the ball right on the end of his big toe. Shit that must have hurt, I thought at the time. In later years, I learned the same trick and became the goal kicker in many of the teams I played with, but not in bare feet.

The Buccaneers were to play against our provincial side, Golden Bay Motueka, later that afternoon. If I recall, the Buccaneers gave Golden Bay Motueka a hell of a thrashing. Reggie Collins played for Golden Bay Motueka. It served him right!

Pintoe's Demise

Pintoe was a huge grey semi-persian tomcat. He lived with the four Crisp brothers next door, most of the time, unless he was on the maraud or in "jail"! The Crisp boys were good blokes and great mates for us.

Pintoe on the other hand was a mean bastard, more so during, and especially after, some of the things we dished out to him. However, the "dishing out" wasn't one way. He was responsible for killing most of our guinea pigs, rabbits, budgies, canaries, pigeons and for peeing and pooping in our sand pit. The total annihilation of my brother Kerry's racing pigeons was the last straw, which for some mysterious reason, happened on the eve of Pintoe's death.

One morning before school we lured Pintoe up onto our windowsill with a dead sparrow tied onto a length of string on the end of a stick. Kerry and I snuck around behind him and threw a blanket over him.

While Sean hauled from inside the bedroom we dragged him kicking, screaming, scratching and biting in through the bedroom window.

Against one wall, we had a portable green painted lowboy with a single door on the front. The middle and only shelf had been removed. It was used to store Sean's *Beano* books, which he had been collecting for years. I wish I knew where that collection was now! We took out the *Beanos* and stuffed Pintoe into the cabinet when we heard someone coming down the hallway, and had to take some urgent remedial action.

Pintoe was as strong as a big kiwi possum, twice as fierce and four times as big. Could have been an All Black, "'cept he couldn't talk but could bite like Richard Lowe," reckoned Kerry some years later. Richard Lowe, an All Black, had gained notoriety many years later for the odd bit of eye gouging and ear biting. Anyway, Pintoe had to be tamed.

The door to the cabinet had one of those ball bearing type closures and Pintoe was trying to push it open from the inside. He would have succeeded had we not turned the cabinet around so that the door was facing hard up against the wall. To our surprise, the back of the cabinet was made of wooden slats and to the small three boy audience, "mad Pintoe" was now in a green jail. He stood there on his hind legs, his front legs clamped around the slats like a tiger in a cage or one of us in jail. The local cop had threatened us with this on many occasions and even gave us a trial run!

Pintoe was hissing and snarling. An impressive but scary sight, even more so, if you were a guinea pig, pigeon, budgie, or in the opposing front row to an All Black forward pack. We gave him a dry Weetbix before we went to school and the odd poke with a stick to settle him down. This was a little taste of what was to come when we came home from school, to keep his mind and throat in mute mode. Turpentine probably would not have worked on this cat's bum, as he was half panther.

At precisely 3.30 p.m., that afternoon Pintoe was going to get his. Or so we thought.

We bashed and banged on the green cabinet and the more we gave him the more resolved he became, probably, to kill us. We rattled sticks across the slats, shone torches full in his face and shook the hell out of his jail. We kept our hands and feet out of the way of his paws and claws, which by now were green with all the paint he had scratched off the walls and bars.

We were going to keep him in jail for another day and then parole him. The treatment we had given him had not weakened his resolve, strength or desire for revenge. It had however, weakened the cabinet! Unknown to us, one of the slats had come loose. Pintoe had gone quiet and on closer inspection, he seemed worn out, lying on his tummy on the floor of his jail. His yellow eyes now mere slits.

All three of us were staring into the wooden green jail when Pintoe made his move. Like a crocodile, he made a sudden flying leap at the bars. We leaped back in fright as Pintoe struck the centre slat, which shattered on impact, and he was free. He roared up one of the curtains to where a top window was fractionally open but the gap was far too small for an escape attempt. He hurled himself down onto Sean's bed, which acted like a trampoline, and this sent him toward Kerry's bed where he peed in mid-flight.

Kerry had launched himself up on top of his wardrobe to get out of the big cat's way and it seemed that Pintoe was also headed in that direction. I felt like diving into Pintoe's ex prison cell. Sean was egging Pintoe on to greater heights of terror and destruction by waving a pillow round and round his head like a lasso. We didn't have long to wait until Pintoe obliged.

Pintoe leapt at a shelf on the wall by Kerry's bed and down fell a plaster of paris statue of the Virgin Mary, which shattered on the wooden floor. The wire and earpiece of Sean's crystal radio set was wrapped around Pintoe's right hind leg. He was now tearing around the floor in circles and then under the beds, upon which we were now jumping up and down, blindly trying to knock him out or squash him. We could feel him belting his head on the bed wire but this did not seem to bother him. He was dragging what was left of the crystal radio set around with him. All of a sudden, he screeched to a halt on the only bit of carpet in the room, snorted and pawed like a bull, and then ran straight at the wall at the end of my bed.

Cats, mean ones like Pintoe, although he would take some beating, can run up wallpaper. What's more, this one actually performed a feat, unheard of since that very afternoon. He actually ran around two walls, six feet off the floor, parallel to the floor, as if on a monorail, totally defying gravity. This feat was aided by the fact that beneath the layers of wallpaper there was a layer of woven scrim that was not well adhered to the wall. I suppose his claws got added traction from this.

We were transfixed, in awe of this great beast. Then with a series of grand leaps he went from the wallpaper to the floor, crashed through the pane glass window, onto the driveway and up and over the ten foot high bamboo fence to the safe haven of "Crisp land." The bastard had beaten us at our own game.

The revenge of the Panther.

That night Kerry lost all twenty of his homing pigeons. They were discovered the next morning, all feet up in their cage up on top of the pump shed. Feathers for miles! Two mornings later, we found Pintoe. Dead of old age we supposed. He was sprawled out on an old sofa bed in our tree hut in the plum tree, stiff as a board.

Someone buried him in the garden under the artichokes but no one had the courage to tell Graham, Dennis, Murray and Roger Crisp next door. It took about a week of nights before they stopped calling Pintoe for dinner.

Tomato Man

There were lots of little things I didn't understand, or things that for some reason didn't make sense to me as a kid growing up in Motueka.

For instance, I was certain that George Stephens was Jewish. His name, however, didn't seem to fit somehow. He had a darkish Mediterranean complexion, as did his kids, and George sure had a big nose. He had the type of nose that many people from that area seemed to have. In fact, his nose was even bigger than my brother Kerry's hooter and that was big enough! He went to the Catholic Church as well. Maybe that was because there was not a synagogue handy, I don't know.

I later found out that George was Lebanese but at the time anyone from the Middle East, even second generation, was "Jewish". Political correctness in any shape or form was not the order of the day. Most people didn't seem to mind these misunderstandings especially when errors were made by kids.

Although not a good simile, it was sort of like believing that Jesus spoke English when he roamed around the place and we were never told at school that in actual fact his native tongue was probably Aramaic.

Anyway, George was a good bloke and a good father to his large family. He always took time out to attend sports days and carted dozens of kids to inter-school footy games in his large car. Not many other parents did this.

He worked as a wharfie and although that was hard physical work, he probably made heaps of money. Mot actually had a pretty busy little harbour and wharf in those days. Ships would come there to be hand loaded with thousands of boxes of apples, eventually destined for England. There were no containers or container ships then and all cargo was loaded by hand.

The wharf job must have only been for the hours that a ship could come in on the tide, get loaded up and then go out again on the same tide. This gave George the time for another little business which consisted of growing vegetables, in particular tomatoes.

He had quite a big block of land in the main street. Out the back of the house he had a little vegetable store, which was packed full of homegrown tomatoes, a set of scales and a pile of brown paper bags. He also had a hot house and could grow tomatoes almost all year round. During the times that our garden was not producing tomatoes, we would be sent out to buy a couple of pound from George which, if I recall correctly, cost about sixpence a pound.

We would go into his little shed and there he'd be, weighing up bags of tomatoes. Our request for two pound would take him about ten minutes as he would do his damdest to get the exact weight by putting them onto the scales one by one. If the last tomato went over the two pound mark he would hunt around for a slightly smaller one to get the weight exactly right. The thing that really intrigued me about George was that once he had the exact weight in the bag he would hand it to us, peer through his bushy eyebrows and say, "Tell your father I gave you good measure."

So what, I thought to myself. Tell him yourself I thought. What was George worried about? Did Dad have something on him? Was he trying reverse psychology and he really had ripped us off after all? Mum sure as hell wasn't going to weigh the bloody things when we got home and if she did, and they were under weight, she would have shrugged it off by thinking that we had eaten one on the way home, which generally was the case! George was on a winner both ways here.

Not only that, the scales were up on the bench, which was about eye level for me, and I could not tell if he had his thumb on the scales or not. He probably had hollowed out weights as well for all I know. Anyway I will never know the answers to those questions as George and Dad are both long gone.

Hindsight is great. In spite of George's "good measure" which I'm sure was always spot on, Mum could well have sent us to buy tomatoes from another "George" on the other side of town.

This George was a professional market gardener. Mum said he had a green thumb and on the occasions we visited him, for other vegetables, I often had a sneak peek at his hands and saw no sign of any green bits.

He might not have had a green thumb but must have had a black bank balance though, as he later bought the Post Office!

Then there was a bloke called Peter, son of Joe. He didn't grow tomatoes and didn't have a green thumb but I thought he too, was Jewish! Alas he was Lebanese as well. Crikey, they were all over the show! He worked in his father's clothing store.

If he'd grown tomatoes there was no way that Mum would have got the chance to send us littlies to buy them from him. My sister Hilary had a bad case of the hots for him and she would have gone and bought his tomatoes day in and day out!

Whoops, I digress a little, but in spite of the fact that the original tomato man has passed away, the other George is alive and well. He must be about a hundred years old but he still flogs his veges at the markets and owns about a quarter of the shops in Mot, as well as the Post Office!

"Peter" owns another quarter of the shops in Mot and Hilary probably kicks herself for not being persistent enough!

P.S. The second George was neither Jewish nor Lebanese. Not even a Catholic, and some say he may well have sneaked into New Zealand from Yugoslavia or somewhere like that when no-one was looking! Who cares and good on him if that's the case!

Ten Bob and A Budgie

As altar boys at the Catholic Church, we often attended weddings. Not by invitation or choice. It was just part of the job. Kerry and I were altar boys for both Sir Pat and Peter Goodman within the space of a year or so. Sir Pat married Hilary and Peter married Irene. These were two wonderful young local ladies.

Peter Goodman gave both Kerry and I a ten bob note each, a lot of money for a small boy in those days. Both notes were rolled up and forced into our Post Office Savings moneyboxes. These moneyboxes were a sod of a thing to break into as they were made of steel. The Post Office had the only key to unlock them. The boxes also had a set of spring-loaded teeth and when you pushed the money in you couldn't get it out. Not even with a knife or screwdriver – believe me, we tried!

When Sir Pat got married, he gave me ten bob and Kerry a budgie! My ten bob went into the moneybox with its mate. Kerry's budgie died about a week later, not because he tried to force it into his moneybox, but for some other reason. Sir Pat gave him another budgie. I did not get another ten bob. However, in years to come I would get the opportunity to work for, and with, Sir Pat and Peter for almost twenty years in their global business empire, Goodman Fielder, so I guess all is forgiven.

My original two ten bob notes resurfaced some thirty years later when Mum passed away. We were sorting out the cupboards at home and came across six moneyboxes. Mine still had the two ten bob notes in it and a few coins.

There were only six moneyboxes, not seven. We laughed when Sean owned up to the fact that when he was thirteen he needed money for a transistor radio to replace his crystal set so he had taken his money box out into Dad's shed and tried to demolish it with a sledge hammer and chisel. That didn't work and nor did putting it out on the street and letting half a dozen cars and a truck run over it. He finally succeeded in opening it by taking it to school and cutting it in half using the band saw in the engineering workshop. "Cut two bloody florins and a shilling in half at the same time," he said. Sean's moneybox would have been the only one that was full at the time.

Backyard Cricket Horgan Style!

Normally we played cricket in the back yard but one day after school we found ourselves out in the park at the bottom of the garden. We had a tennis ball, a bat and a couple of wooden apple boxes for wickets. The park was unofficially called the "cricket ground" and was about five acres in area. We were playing our normal game of "tip and he runs" or "tippenny runs", which meant that if the ball got the slightest touch on the bat you had to run.

You had a bowler at each end and a single batsman. The ball could be bowled from either end of the pitch, depending on where the batsman ended up. A six, or six runs, could only be scored if you hit the ball over the fence on the full but then you were automatically out. The only time you could score six runs and keep batting, was by hitting the fence on the full and having the ball bounce back into play.

All families seemed to have their own sets of rules and the game was played in back yards, streets and parks across New Zealand, Australia, India, England, Pakistan, South Africa and so on, so there is no need to go into too much detail. The basics of the game are the same world wide except for the odd idiosyncrasy such as "the littlest, the youngest and girls bat last"!

The ball was usually a tennis ball, but every now and then, the bowler let fly with a concealed rock, apple, or over-ripe tomato just to keep you on your toes! These missiles were body-liners. It would usually be me who was on the receiving end of the rocks and the tomatoes and they were "chucked" at full throttle, face high.

We were playing on the side of the cricket ground next to a ten-foot high, honey-suckle infested, thorn bush hedge. Sean reckoned he had made a hundred runs, which was questionable. (But who were Kerry and I to question it, as we were smaller than he was?) He was getting bored with batting so he deliberately slogged the ball for a six. The ball went up and over the hedge.

Trouble was that the grass in the paddock over the hedge was three feet high and the ball was going to take some finding. As usual, I had to climb over the hedge to find it. I clambered over the fence and into the paddock. It really was like trying to find a needle in a haystack and Sean and Kerry were yelling out at me to hurry up and find the "bloody ball".

Next thing I am flat on my back. God knows how long I was there. Then I was back on my feet wandering around in a daze in the long grass. It was now quite late in the evening, probably a couple of hours after the ball had been hit over the hedge.

Then Sean and Kerry arrived. It must have been tea time and they had been sent to find me. They had earlier gone home in disgust without even bothering to call me. They said they did but I didn't hear them. No bloody wonder! Apparently, Sean had the shits that I had not found the ball and had blindly thrown the bat up and over the hedge to give me a hurry-up. The bat had hit me on the full, right behind the left ear, and pole axed me.

I had a hell of a lump behind my ear, oozing yellow coloured stuff and this went on for days. "Could not have been brains," Sean kept telling Kerry as they taunted me over the incident during the following weeks.

Neither Sean nor Kerry ever owned up to having thrown the bat. Mum and Dad never knew of the incident as I was under threat of death, or even worse, if I ever told them about it. One day I will get even but that was almost fifty years ago. Although they say that time heals all, I can assure you that it does not and one day, they will get theirs!

Hot Head

Every year we went on holiday. It was a grand event.

The Post Office had a couple of rental units at a beach called Kaiteriteri. Dad worked for the Post Office and so the subsidised rental for these units was quite cheap.

Kaiteriteri was eight miles from Motueka. Access was via a winding, hilly gravel road. The beach was in a sheltered bay and had beautiful golden sand and the tide never seemed to go out.

We used to stay there for two weeks in late October, early November when Dad took some holidays and we had to go to school in a bus. This was a big deal. Normally we were there for the celebration of Guy Fawkes Night on the 5th of November. This was a traditional celebration that commemorated Guy Fawke's dismal failure to blow up England's

Houses of Parliament. I always thought that we, my brothers and I, could have done a better job than he did. Anyone could buy fireworks of any description in those days and you could buy them from most shops, weeks before the 5th of November. The crackers or bangers came in four sizes. Tom Thumbs were the smallest cracker, about one inch long and a sixteenth of an inch thick. The next was about the size of a cigarette, and then came the "penny banger", which was the size of a shotgun cartridge. There was another larger one again but it was too expensive to buy and because two penny bangers could do the same damage as one of these, it was silly to buy them.

You could hold the small Tom Thumb crackers in your fingertips as they exploded. To do this with the bigger sizes was not on unless you did not want your fingers any more. Sometimes when you lit the fuse to a penny banger it refused to ignite. The fuse burnt down and died. With not much caution, you would approach the cracker to get a visual to see if the wick was still slow burning or if it had gone out. Quite often they were duds. If so you bent the cracker in half and one side would split to expose the black gunpowder. Holding the bent cracker by the two sealed ends between your forefinger and thumb, you would apply flame to the exposed gunpowder.

The result was a whooshing gust of red-hot gunpowder. This was quite spectacular at night, and even more so, if you pulled the stunt in the local picture theatre, where unbelievably, the patrons used to smoke. The gunpowder sometimes took a while to ignite and close visual inspection of the half-broken cracker at this point is not recommended!

We would use fire crackers for all sorts of tricks. A favourite was using the big penny bangers as ammo in catapults and shanghais. Another trick was to light a penny banger and drop it into an unsuspecting, soon to be ex-mate's, pants pocket.

I personally went off fireworks a bit after our holiday the year I turned eight.

It was at Kaiteriteri on Guy Fawkes evening that the trick of "bending the cracker open" backfired. It was not yet dark and I found an amenities block in the beach camping ground in which to trial some of the crackers and Catherine wheels. The acoustics for such an exercise are perfect in a concrete building with a steel roof.

The first penny banger I lit seemed to be a dud, and so I bent it in half and lit the exposed gunpowder. It was still a dud. The Chinese had ripped me off I thought. I turned the exposed, slightly smouldering cracker towards my face to see what was going on when all of a sudden all hell broke loose.

Two streams of red-hot gunpowder shot out of the cracker. One went up my left nostril and the other one up my right. I dropped the still burning cracker and clutched my nose in agony. Shit! The burning cracker then fell into the paper bag containing the rest of my fireworks. I had saved for months to get these. Catherine wheels, strings of half crackers, Tom Thumbs, penny bangers, skyrockets, jumping jacks and flowerpots were in that bag. My bloody nose felt like a red-hot poker had been stuffed up each nostril.

Then the rest of the fire works went off. I was screaming and jumping up and down. The shed, which before was almost dark, was now going crazy with colours whirling around from the Catherine wheels and sky rockets whizzing round crashing off the walls and ceiling. Crackers, still on their strings were going off like machine guns. Jumping jacks were rattling around the room, and to top it off the little multi-coloured flower pots were giving the effect that I was inside a bloody kaleidoscope.

The room filled with sparks and smoke. Under normal circumstances it would have been my own private fireworks display but it wasn't a normal circumstance. My fucking nose was on fire and now I could hardly breathe or see. Blinded by the lights, I couldn't find the door and the smoke was choking the shit out of me.

It died down after a short while and I found the door and stumbled out of the shed trying to find a hose to squirt up my nostrils. My clothes reeked of smoke for weeks even after numerous washings. I was surprised that Mum never said anything about it.

I never told anyone about this little escapade simply because of my embarrassment. On top of that, I had numerous nosebleeds over the ensuing days and kept coughing up soot. I couldn't blow my nose because it hurt so much. My nose ran frequently. For days, two sooty black snot lines ran down from my nostrils to my top lip. My jersey sleeve was filthy from wiping it away. I simply rolled up my right sleeve between wipes. Yuck!

Back When A Smoke Was A Smoke

Fifty years ago, the Motueka district was New Zealand's only tobacco growing area. The crop was grown, dried and graded on the many farms that grew it. It was then trucked off to either of the two large tobacco factories for further processing. Thirty years ago, however, tobacco was replaced with other crops such as kiwi fruit and grapes. Apples and hops are also grown in the district and have been for over a hundred years.

The Motueka district has very fertile soil, cold clear days in winter, balanced rainfall, and long hot summers. Almost any fruit or vegetables grow there as well as rumours of the odd plot of marijuana.

Fishing is a booming industry with large fleets of ocean-going trawlers. Oysters, scallops, and other shellfish abound and whitebait can be caught by recreational fishermen. When we were kids however, apples, tobacco and hops were the main income earners for the district. Planting, harvesting and pruning these crops brought a seasonal population growth of thousands to the town from all over New Zealand and from around the world. Many stayed on and the town has now grown to twelve thousand.

Families well established for generations owned land which was not Maori lease. Names such as Fry, Drummond, Rowling, Inglis, Cederman, Grooby and Thorn. Two types of tobacco were grown. The lesser of the two being Burleigh, which had a long narrow leaf and was air-dried, as opposed to its counterpart which was kiln dried. Harvesting took place from late January through to March and many of the seasonal workers stayed on after the tobacco to pick pip and stone fruit. Hops were harvested for a short period in February/March and in those days were picked by hand from the vines, which were cut down only minutes before picking. Mainly local women and school kids picked hops. I can still smell the sticky sweet scent of the hops as we stripped them from the vines and that was fifty years ago. The manual harvesting of hops stopped in the late 1950s when mechanical harvesters took over. At the same time, the number of individual growers declined and other farms increased their acreage of hops under cultivation.

From time to time, we used to pinch a few fully-grown Burleigh tobacco plants. We would hang them out to dry, slice up the leaves, roll them into cigars and smoke them. Sometimes we would get hold of the more common type of tobacco, slice it up and make our own cigarettes. At one stage, we even grew a few plants in the back garden.

Our hand made cigars and cigarettes were pretty volatile to say the least. If you did manage to inhale the smoke one of two things would happen. You would either get as high as a kite or become violently ill. Many kids gave up smoking forever when they tried our homemade cigarettes.

The symptoms and aftermath of some of these "grow, dry, make your own smokes" could be horrifying. If you couldn't handle them your face would turn the whitest of whites, then yellow, then red, then white again. In this final white stage, you would become violently ill. So ill that you thought you were going to die. Worse than the worst hangover a young man in his late teens might have after his first encounter with alcohol.

After a couple of seasons of making our own smokes we got into the real thing and pinched a packet or two from the local department store. Sort of like a department come supermarket store. It may have been called Woolworths. The large food stores were not known as supermarkets and sold food only. The store layout was so different in the 1950s to what it is today and personal service was available at most times, unavoidable unfortunately.

The counters were about four foot six inches high and we were about four foot high. As you walked an aisle, you would have to figure out where the tobacco was positioned. One would then walk as close to the counter as possible so that the shop assistant could not see you from behind it. You would then stick your hand up and over the edge of the counter and grope around for what you hoped was a packet of Capstan Cork or Capstan Plain, because that is what Dad smoked, grab it and run like hell out of the shop. Then boys would sit in their tree hut and smoke the lot!

On one particular solo mission to Woolworths, having being forced to do the dirty work by the threat of a thrashing from my slightly older brothers and their mates, I went through the routine. All went well until I got home to the tree hut to find, that I had pinched pipe tobacco and not smokes! I had to go back and either swap the pipe tobacco or pinch a pipe. I pinched the pipe. The side effects however, of smoking pipe tobacco stopped me from smoking until I was nineteen and my brothers have not smoked at all ever since that day in the tree hut. I do not recommend taking up smoking a pipe as a way of giving up cigarettes.

In hindsight, I am not proud of the forays into Woolworths. That was bad and I knew damn well that it was a huge step towards purgatory!

The alternative to smoking tobacco-based products was willow root. Yes, the tree from which came cricket bats and aspirin. In the Motueka area, thousands of willow trees grew along the banks of the rivers. As the river banks erode, the willow roots are exposed and in the sun, the roots dry out. Selecting some, the diameter of a regular cigarette, we would cut them into lengths similar to that of a cigarette. The root is porous and all you do is light up and take a drag. The inhaled smoke can get a bit hot but other than that, I guess, willow root smokes would get smokers through a period when they didn't have the real thing. Not only that, I cannot remember ever having a headache after smoking willow root. I have often wondered if that was anything to do with the aspirin content.

Wallpaper

I think our house was built about the time Dad was born, 1912. High ceilings, huge rooms and a hallway you could drive a car down without whacking the wing mirrors on the walls. The house was wall papered throughout. For various reasons the bedroom where Sean, Kerry and I slept seemed to get a fresh wallpapering every couple of years.

The internal walls of the house were made of timber studs, which were clad with what was known as sarking. This was half-inch thick timber boards coated with a sort of a rubberised plaster. Over the plaster was a layer of woven sacking type material called scrim. The scrim was tacked on to the walls and then the wallpaper was glued to it. After about twenty layers of wallpaper over wallpaper some of the tacks that held the scrim to the wall came away. This left air bubbles or bulges between the wall and the now cardboard-like wall covering. That probably held the house up! One of these bulges was between my bed and the wall.

On many occasions, we would climb out the bedroom window late in the evening taking a pillowcase with us to raid some of the neighbours' fruit trees and grape vines. Then we would have a midnight fruit feast in our bedroom. The biggest problem was the disposal of the seeds, pips and stones from the fruit.

Just below the mattress height we would slit the wallpaper with a pocket knife. As the paper was no longer glued to the wall it acted like a pocket for all the seeds and pips. If you looked at the wall under the bed, however, there was a rather large bulge. From time to time, we would cut another slit in the wallpaper at the top of the skirting board and all the seeds would tumble out. These would be disposed of "over Eric's".

"Over Eric's" meant that we would chuck the rubbish over the next-door neighbour's fence. Eric was the fat son who lived there. The bloke we thought was a girl because his mother often dressed him as one.

We would then put clear Sellotape over the bottom slit and start the process again.

I recall that once we didn't cut the bottom slit for about a year and one day I noticed a couple of tiny green leaves protruding out of the slit beside the bed. On further inspection, it was a small plum tree, which had somehow germinated down at the bottom of the pile of seeds.

The old house was fairly damp all year round. I guess that the seed must have sprouted roots in other decaying seeds and pips and sent down a taproot through the wall. Somehow bypassing the bottom plate, and into the earth beneath the floorboards.

We quickly ripped out the seedling but in hindsight, it would have been great to see the tree grow up the wall inside the bedroom. "A sort of indoor pot plant." We could have cultivated it and grown our own plums in the bedroom.

Mum would have taken a dim view of it but Dad would have seen the humorous side. I doubt if he would have liked the idea of our watering it though. We could have done this however, by squirting the hose under the house every once and a while or by peeing on it!

The Neighbours' Neighbours and The Hunt Girls

Next door to us lived the Crisps: Graham, Dennis, Murray, Roger and Pintoe, "the cat of cats."

On the opposite side, most of the time, were the Blanchards. "She", (said Mum) had a son-called Eric and we thought Eric was a girl because sometimes "She" would dress poor Eric in a dress. In dress or pants he still looked like a girl with curly white hair and a fat girl's build. He was, however, overly tall and wide for his age.

The Wallers lived on the other side of Eric. They had two sons, Brian and Graham Bond. At the time I could never figure out why the kids' surname was different than their parents. No one ever said anything about it so it was best to leave it be. Brian was "Bondy" of "Bondy's Belching Club" or the "BBC". Brian and Graham were like chalk and cheese. Brian was really big and tough and had a powerful slug gun and Graham was skinny and played honky tonk piano and flew real aeroplanes.

Rumour had two lesbian high school teachers living on the other side of Bondy but no one ever said that aloud. Anything outside the norm in those days was not a discussion point and therefore taboo. I didn't even know what a lesbian was then and the rumour was probably just exactly that. Next to the teachers the Bowdens lived in a modern house set well back from the road on a block of land twice the size of ours.

On the other side of the Crisps lived the Hodges and old man Hodge had a shotgun and a black Labrador called Sport. Sport lived forever, and used to wait at the front gate for the paper every night.

Next to Hodges came the Wilkes. Old man Wilkes was a local bank manager known as "Cocky". At the time I thought that his nickname must have been derived from his dick. He was short and fat. He also had a gun. It was rumoured to be a .38. I never knew exactly what a .38 was but reckoned that Bondy would have loved to get his hands on it. I think the gun belonged to the bank in case they were robbed. Mr Wilkes kept it at home in a little wooden box. Anyway, I seriously doubted that his nickname could have originated from dick prowess. He somehow just didn't seem the type. His main claim to fame was the rumour that he shot cats marauding within his beloved vegetable garden with the .38. No one could ever prove it and no one would ever mention it aloud because he was the bank manager. In those days, the bank manager was God. How things have changed. Cocky had far too much influence in the town for anyone to dare get on his bad side.

Then came the Thorpes who were newcomers and had three girls and a son called Jeremy. A name which had "sissy" written all over it, but he wasn't. The Silks lived in the house next to Thorpes.

Then came Miss Black, one half of the famous "Ingram and Black" duo, the state school primary teachers. It is quite odd actually, how that in Motueka, most of the female schoolteachers lived in our street and were not married. There were also the nuns of course but they did not live in our street thank God!

Owen Grooby lived on the other side of Miss Black. His was almost the last house before the T intersection of the main street. On the corner opposite Groobys was the original Goodman estate house and bakery.

Across the road from Thorpes lived Mr Duncan or "Dunk", the local traffic cop and he was fat. I mean really fat. Mrs Duncan was a little lady who looked like a dumpling but she was really nice and had rosy, rosy cheeks.

The Stairs lived next to Dunk and they were a mysterious mob. Mr Stair used to give me half a crown to mow his lawns with his motor mower and his petrol. I used to take his mower home and mow our lawns as well, also using his petrol. We never had a motor mower. He probably saw me do it but never said anything about it. We never saw much of the Stairs except when Mr Stair had to rescue us from the odd prank gone wrong. It seemed that he never had a job and they always had the blinds pulled down in their windows. However, he must have had a peephole in the curtains.

Opposite our house was an empty block of land and next to that lived Michael Thomas and the Inwoods. They were somehow connected. This house was soon to become a doctor's surgery, very handy for Mum who visited the doctor regularly. You can probably understand why!

Dotted further down the street on our side were other notable families such as the Craigs. They had two daughters, Stephanie and Julie, who went to the Catholic school. Stephanie had a crush on my brother Kerry and I'm sure it was then that Kerry made up his mind to be a priest and made it public, especially to Stephanie!

Dr Thompson lived way down toward the end of the street and he had a huge double storey house and a swimming pool. They had three daughters, and three sons, including twins, Hamish and Simon. They were sort of like Tweedle Dum and Tweedle Dee.

Another family of Horgans lived almost opposite Dr Thompson at number 89. They were not Catholics and not related to us in any way, I hoped.

They were a scruffy mob and the old man, Tom, was a motor mechanic, not that there was anything wrong with that of course. I thought they had no right to live in our street, as we were there first! They probably thought the same about us on all counts.

At the very end of the street lived the McGlashens who owned heaps of land and had one of the largest hop plantations in the district. They had a son called Kim, which I thought was a girl's name.

An Irish bloke called Doug Shaw lived opposite the McGlashens. Doug and Dad built a little cabin boat and often went deep-sea fishing.

Over the road from the Bowden's, lived Grandma Hewitt and our Protestant mate Piers Lummis. I was never quite sure how Piers, or Lummy as we called him, was related to Grandma Hewitt and didn't really care. Lummy's father had a butcher shop and Lummy had other brothers as well but they all lived on the other side of town. Again, I don't know what happened there and didn't care about that either. He was our mate and it was none of our business.

Right next door to Grandma and Lummy lived the notorious Hunt girls. Dawn, Patty, Phyllis (and Terrence). The girls should have been boys and Terrence should have been a girl, so Mum reckoned. I don't really know what happened here, when these kids were born or just prior to that. Something had obviously gone radically wrong at conception time.

Patty and Phyllis were twins. Double trouble. Dawn was the oldest. Mum said on a couple of occasions that Dawn was a mealy mouthed, spiteful girl and had a vocab worse than the devil's. We were shocked that Mum would ever say such a thing. Dawn could easily hold her own with a shanghai, catty or the odd well-aimed rock. She was probably quite a good kid but girls were not meant to fight with shanghais, rocks and fists. That was a boy's domain!

Phyllis had mousey blond hair and Patty's hair was red. We often saw the twins belting each other up. Patty was a fiery bird with heaps of freckles and was a good scrapper. Mrs Hunt was also a redhead and Patty was her image. I don't know if Mrs Hunt was a scrapper though!

Pa Hunt wasn't a bad sort of a bloke and he always nodded his head when he biked past our place on his way home from work. Behind the nod, he was probably thinking something very different to what we thought. He seemed to keep much to himself except when we bailed up his daughters or he caught us beating up Terrence in the street.

Rock fights with the Hunt girls were common and Pa Hunt would come roaring out of his shed with a shovel or broom, trying to fend off our marble and rock missiles, hand thrown, or from catapults. I don't really think his daughters approved of his interference in the street fights because they believed they could beat us in a three on three!

We had their match, however, because our mate Lummy, who lived on the other side of them, would help us catch Pa Hunt and his three Amazon warriors in a cross fire, forcing them back into their driveway. We used rubbish tin lids as shields from the stones and rocks the Amazons threw at us.

I admit that I never walked down the Hunt girls' side of the street when I went to visit our mate, Lummy and his Grandma. I was scared shitless of them and always thought that if I walked past their house they would abduct and torture me, especially Dawn.

Lummy and my brother Sean built a two storey hut out the back of Grandma Hewitt's house. It was more a fortress than a hut and it had a concealed trap door in the lower floor, which led to an underground hideaway or "jail". Rumour has it that one rainy day Dawn Hunt was lured into the hut on the pretence of a truce and then locked down in the jail for the day! When it rained, the jail used to flood.

Poole Street was certainly the place to live in if you wanted variety and hated peace and quiet!

I often wonder what happened to all these people, what they have done and where they are now. I am sure that many have stayed in the area, probably because of the lifestyle. Of those who left Motueka, have they prospered? Have they found a better place to live and bring up their own children? I suggest that both the people who stayed and the ones who left have all become successful, simply because of the diversity of their upbringing in Motueka.

What was so special about growing up in Mot? There was a great sense of community — everyone helped everyone else — and as much as the Catholic and Protestant kids fought, most of it was for effect. I am sure of this because there were no religious boundaries when the chips were down. Yet there were great extremes in the town. The rich and the poor, large and small families, loners and the lonely.

Yet it was the sense of community that broke down the social barriers. It is certainly true to say that many prominent people were raised in the town. Although I do not have concrete evidence, I believe that the percentage of these was much higher than the national average.

There are many success stories of people from Motueka and these are not only based on wealth or fame. Some very prominent, wealthy and high profile people live or lived in the town and surrounding areas of Motueka. The Goodman brothers, the Talleys, quite a number of ex-All Blacks, Guy Bowers, Bill Taylor and Trevor Morris, and New Zealand Cricket reps such as brothers Ian and Barry Hampton and Bevan Congdon. There were even a couple of ex-prime Ministers, Rowling and Holyoake. Note how I put him last!

My brother Sean and I visit Motueka every October to spend a few weeks whitebaiting. I hear stories of many of my old friends and classmates when I return for the whitebait season. While they may not all be famous or wealthy, what they have in common is that they lead rich and fulfilling lives and seem happy and contented. Is there a better measure of success?

The town has grown four fold. It is rare that on my visits back home that I recognise any of the people we knew when we were young. I have never run into the Hunt Girls. Probably just as well!

First Love

I was ten years old. We were at the convent school. The convent catered daily for all those Catholic kids in the area who could get there within a reasonable time frame.

The other Catholic kids from farms around the district more than ten miles away, had to be content with attending their own local state primary schools. These were located in little towns and settlements such as Thorpe, Tasman, Brooklyn, Mapua and Tapawera.

Unluckily for these country Catholic kids, their religion dictated that every fourth Sunday they had to attend classes at the Convent school in Motueka. I reckoned that this was not the Pope's dictatorial but rather the local priest and nuns' law. Possibly a vain hope that these kids' parents were rich. They were by many "townies" standards. The possible plan was that the parents of these kids would bring them into town for the early morning mass. This could help swell the coffers by donating to the twice-passed around plate during the mass.

I had noticed that the green felted offertory plates were one of the most important parts of the mobile mass. As altar boys, we accompanied the local parish priest and nuns to a mass in either Ngatimoti or Mapua every other fourth Sunday of the month. In preparing for such visits, you could forget the wine or the unconsecrated communion hosts but not the plates. I recall also that the rural "take" consisted of coins and the odd note higher in denomination than the coins and lack of notes in the collections in the town masses. Not only that, the plates that accompanied the mobile masses were not the same as the flat wooden green felt covered plates used in the town churches. They were woven wicker baskets with sides on!

At Christmas time there were also masses held at a beach house at Kaiteriteri. It was quite a tourist spot and forty thousand people would come to our town to spend Christmas. Many of these tourists were Catholics and some were reasonably wealthy. The church services were crammed as were the plates. There were heaps of masses held over the Christmas holiday period at Kaiteriteri Beach and in the two Catholic churches in the township of Motueka.

At the town masses you would steer clear of sitting next to Sir Pat Goodman or Peter Goodman as Dad's two bob, (florin or twenty cents), or half crown (twenty five cents) looked pretty miserable in comparison to their generous ten bob or one pound note.

It all got out of hand in the end and just like taxes, the costs of running the priest's car and feeding the nuns jumped a bit. Little yellow envelopes were sent to all Catholic families. They had your name and number on them. Dad had to put money in the envelope each week. "Big Brother" was alive and well.

Anyway, after that little digression, her name was Rosalie. Her parents had an apple orchard at Mapua. The minute I saw her I fell in love with her and I hoped the feeling was mutual. She had blue, blue eyes and fair hair, cut as if a pudding bowl had been placed on her head, but the style was beautifully done!

Each time mass was scheduled for Mapua you could be sure that I would be there as one of the altar boys just to catch a glimpse of Rosalie. Every fourth Sunday I would also have some excuse to be down at the convent school to cop another glimpse. Excuses for being there ranged from feeding the parish priest's chooks to cleaning his car or mowing the lawns, Sunday or not!

Rosalie's mother was a different kettle of fish and I distinctly knew that she knew that I more than fancied Rosalie. Rosalie was her mother and father's pride and joy. I read it on their faces, which silently spelled "Our Rosalie will never be allowed to see this kid from a poor lower class family and she is totally out of bounds". In later years, I'd see that same look on other mothers' faces more than once. However, it made no difference and where possible I never let it become an obstacle.

A relationship with Rosalie however, was doomed right from the start but I didn't give up. For years, I tried to contact her even when they sent her away to a private boarding school and then to teachers training college. All to no avail.

Eleven years later, when I was twenty-one I was walking down Lambton Quay, one of the main streets of Wellington. It had been raining and was cold, windy, and just past five o'clock on a winter's evening. Rain and wind was normal for Wellington. I had finished work and was walking to my car.

I stopped at a lights controlled pedestrian crossing. There, standing right beside me was Rosalie. She was side on to the crossing and me as if she was pondering as to cross or not.

She was wearing an expensive fawn mid-length mohair coat, unbuttoned. She had a cream woollen scarf and a trendy multi-coloured knitted wool hat, in pastel shades. Her now honey blond hair, shoulder length, fell out beneath the wool hat and her eyes were still blue, blue. She was no longer just pretty but absolutely beautiful.

She was wearing light tan casual shoes and clear nylons. Her legs had that tanned, athletic look but not overly done. The sort of legs that models would die for and that men would pay dearly to see more of. I had heard that description somewhere before and it just seemed to fit.

Her breasts were firm and beautifully contoured beneath a light woollen jumper and she wasn't wearing, and didn't need to wear, a bra. Her chin and neckline were of God's best design and her perfect lips wore a faint touch of pink.

I had changed as well and was handsome and trim so Mum said, but I was still poor. My time would come I hoped. I was married and so was she, she said.

It's strange how you remember those things and I also remember thinking at the time how jealous I was of her husband. He must have been rich or very handsome but in hindsight, her mother must have approved of him and so I thought he must have been only rich.

I saw a tear or two in her eyes and although we exchanged a few short greetings and words about not much, her eyes said everything. I'm sure mine did as well. I detected a little pain or sorrow in her eyes and I wanted to ask what it was or why it was or what had happened, or how could anyone have caused her any pain.

I knew and she knew that perhaps her Mum had cost us something special. Or was it Rosalie and me? Did we not try hard enough? She told me that over the years, she had thought of me often. I told her how hard I tried to contact her and yet she already knew that, she said. We didn't try hard enough to find each other before we made other commitments.

We stood silent then for many cycles of light changes, red, green, orange, walk, don't walk, without talking. Just looking at each other or staring out into space and looking at the ground.

Other pedestrians came and went and when cars streamed by on green lights and screeched to a halt on red, we missed it all. Time stood still and almost seemed to tell us to wind back the clock a year or two.

We didn't need to talk aloud. It seemed that just being in the same space was generating unsaid conversation. I was hurting so much inside and I had never felt that way before.

We never physically touched or shook hands. We just walked away. I crossed one way and she the other. I walked towards my car and then perhaps a further twenty paces after I had crossed the street I could not stop myself turning to see her just one more time. It was like extra sensory perception and she did the same at the exact same time. I wanted desperately to run to her and hold her and kiss her and I knew she wanted me to as well but I was glued to the pavement.

I took my hand from my pocket to give a small wave. It was meant to have signalled that I wanted to see her again soon. However, a bus went by and blocked my vision and after it had gone, she had vanished.

I wanted to search for her but did not know where to start. She had a new name and I did not know what it was.

Over the years, I have often visited my home town of Motueka. The main highway still passes through the tiny township of Mapua and right past the front gate to the apple orchard where Rosalie lived. I do not know if her parents are still alive. I do not know who owns the farm now. I have often been tempted to go in and find out. Perhaps I will one day.

I hope she is happy but after our brief meeting on a windy Wellington street, I heard that her marriage, like mine, had ended. However, thirty-five years have passed since that day and they say that time heals all. It doesn't really.

It is funny reminiscing. My brothers and sisters and even my mother did not approve of my ten-year old's crush on Rosalie. They often teased me about her and even gave her a nickname that so upset me.

Rosalie obtained her degree and became a teacher. She is probably still teaching, or maybe she has a flower shop, who knows?

The Bike Converters

For a while, we had too many bikes lying around the place so Dad built us a bike shed. It was modelled on a small version of the bike shed at the public school opposite the park, out the back of our place. The old man never really seemed to ask and probably didn't care where all the bikes came from, or to where they disappeared!

I was twelve and in my last year at the convent primary school and Sean was in fourth form at high school. Kerry, the brother in between us was away at boarding school. I probably would not have been given all this practical experience in bike recycling if Kerry had been home. Even then I probably only got it because Sean needed a "gofer".

Sean used to weld bike frames together end to end and build tandems. Tandems needed two sets of most parts except for wheels and so there was the odd bike or two lying around the town missing a seat or handlebars.

One of the handlebar-less bikes was tricked up with an old wooden steering wheel instead of handlebars. It was a really beaut bike and sure as hell, a show stopper. Another bike had coil springs added to cut-away front forks. This bike was thirty years ahead of its time but a pig of a thing to ride.

Now and again, I would ride the steering wheeled bike to school. In those days every six months the local traffic cop would visit all the schools to do a safety check on the kid's bikes. All bikes had to have a certificate of fitness. The certificate covered brakes, lights, mudguards, tyre grip etc. Each bike was issued with a triangular sticker. Green stickers were a pass and pink stickers were a fail. The stickers were stuck onto the frame strut, which connected the seat to the pedal sprocket.

If your bike failed the test then you were given six months to fix the problem. This was not a big issue as all we would do was strip the bike, paint the frame a different colour and change the serial number with a metal punch. Or we could file the number off altogether! The final change was to throw some water onto the pass sticker on someone else's bike and re-glue it onto the new refurbished bike.

We were at the small Catholic school and as mentioned earlier, the public primary school was just across the park from where we lived. Sometimes if it was raining when school got out, some parents from well off families would come and pick the kids up in their cars. The kids would leave their bikes in the bike racks. Sometimes the next morning, some of the stickers would be missing from the bikes left at the public school overnight, or swapped for pink stickers, time permitting! We had quite a supply of green stickers.

Sometimes a whole bike or bikes would go missing, or parts thereof. We noticed this when we were borrowing stickers. We wondered if there was another bunch of kids out there, recycling, so to speak, in a much bigger way than we were! Or was that just a rumour?

The recycled bikes would mysteriously show up at Christmas time as presents for the poorer kids in town. New bikes would be made up from parts. Numbers and colours changed, seats swapped over etc, so that original bikes would never be recognised. Catholic kids needed bikes more than Protestant kids because Catholic kids had further to go to school. Although this seemed a reasonable explanation for "recyclers" it was not really cricket I suppose. The practice was sort of half way between a venial and a mortal sin!

It's strange really, in that I never recall people reporting that a bike had been pinched or borrowed for a year or two. Probably because that sort of thing "just didn't happen" in the town in those days so it never was reported.

Anyway, the day I rode the bike with the steering wheel to school just happened to be the day that the local cop decided to do his bike inspection. He almost had a heart attack when he saw the bike. In his thirty years of bullying kids whose bikes were about to be issued with a pink sticker, he had never encountered such a thing.

Sister Gabriel was as mad as a hornet and boy, was I in for it. I blamed Sean who was at high school and out of her reach. Sister Gabriel was the sort of head teacher whose school had to be the best of all the schools in the district, and had to be first in everything. Not only that, she reckoned that the public schools in the area were attended by a bunch of pagans and heathens. That they would never be able to compete with the convent, simply because they were non-Catholics. That they did not have God's help and backing in the way that her charges did!

In hindsight, it is mind boggling when I think of some of the bullshit we had drummed into us at that school in the way of religious teachings and Catholicism in general. I am pleased to learn that in recent years the Church has mellowed a bit. I am grateful, however, at having the convent school education as my grounding but I do feel that the religious segment was often a little over the top.

Anyway, this was Sister Gabriel's first pink sticker, and I was the "stickee". She certainly got a first in this one I thought at the time.

The local parish priest had a different view of the incident and thought that Sean's bike with a steering wheel was innovative and quite novel. "Where in the laws of the country, does it state that a pushbike has to have handlebars as opposed to a steering wheel?" he said.

It was just as well that the local traffic cop was not a Catholic because the priest used the example of Sean's bike as the basis for one of his sermons. Something along the lines that Christ put us upon this earth to improve our lot and the lot of those less fortunate than us. When he got that far I thought he was going to spill the beans about the missing bikes. How they mysteriously showed up as Christmas presents for Catholic school kids, but he didn't. He knew though because he knew all the secrets of the Catholic kids via the veiled box in the church!

He went on to say that by thinking outside the nine dots, we improve things for everyone. Do things differently to achieve better results. The bike certainly did do this.

- *It was easier to steer.*
- *You could ride it with three passengers, one on the bar, one on the carrier and one on the steering wheel.*
- *You could ride it "no hands" easier than a bike with handlebars.*
- *It was a lot easier to ride backwards.*
- *You could park it anywhere.*
- *To stop people pinching it all you had to do was undo a wing nut and take the steering wheel with you whenever you left the bike somewhere.*

Incidentally, he added, "There seems to be a gang of yet to be apprehended bike-nappers in the district." He then turned to stare down from the pulpit directly at Sean and me. We were desperately trying to slide down in the seat of the pew in the very back row.

Christmas Day At The Horgans'

Lead Up

The day before Christmas my brother Kerry, sister Veronica and I would dig out potholes in the gravel road that ran to the highway from a large field of peas currently being harvested. The trucks piled high with loads of peas still on the vines, would trundle by on their way to the Unilever factory some four miles away. As the wheels hit our potholes, great clumps of peas fell to the road. We snaffled them up and bundled them into sugar bags. We would then tear home on our bikes, laden with the bags of peas and begin the task of shelling them and giving the neighbours a share. The neighbours thought that the peas came from our own garden. Mum turned a blind eye, grateful for the injection of extra food for the next day's dinner, I guess. All the other vegetables would come from our own garden but we never seemed to grow enough peas.

The Mass

No Christmas present until after mass was a bit tough so we all wanted to go to midnight mass but were not allowed because we were "too little". Therefore, when we were very young we attended the 7:00am session and then hurried home to see what Santa had left for us.

I do recall, however, when I was about 18 years old and had been going to midnight mass for some years and like a lot of other "good Catholics", a term for regular mass goers, we poured out of the pubs and went to church!

Motueka with its glorious weather and beautiful beaches was a resort area. The population grew from about 3,000 to about 40,000 at Christmas. Most of the visitors were from the city of Christchurch, some five hours drive south. Christchurch does not have beaches as such. So the annual trek north for the holidays was a must for many cantabrians. Many of these were Catholics.

The Sermon

Christmas sermons were generally pretty light and all about giving. With all the holidaymakers around there would be a few more pounds in the plate. The church was packed and people were twenty deep outside the front door and much the same at the sanctuary end and at each Gothic window. Somehow, this particular year I managed to get a seat towards the back of the church. It was right next to a drunken cantabrian holidaymaker. This bloke was pretty pissed and sat on the pew, leaning on me and alternately what could have been his wife on the other side of him.

After about five minutes, he went to sleep. Then he started snoring. During the first part of the mass there was quite a competition between the priest and drunk. As the drunk snored louder, the priest would speak louder. This little game went on until it was time for the sermon.

The priest, who incidentally, was a member of Alcoholics Anonymous, went up to the pulpit to give his Christmas sermon.

Shock and horror! The priest in his normal quiet monotone voice announced that this sermon was to be about hell and the evils of the demon drink, and what the consequences of this combination would be for Catholics in the after life. He had noticed the location of the drunk sitting next to me, just prior to the sermon.

The drunk snored on, louder and softer, louder and softer and the priest with his fire and brimstone sermon responded with the same voice fluctuation. In the end the priest got really pissed off with the drunk. In a quiet tone he said, "All those people who want to go to hell when they die," and then at the top of his voice, continued, "stand up!"

The drunk got such a fright at the volume of the priest's last two words, obviously the only ones he'd heard, and jumped to his feet. Quite startled, he looked around at everyone else still seated. Then he looked at the priest and said, "I don't know what this is all about Father, but you and I are the only ones standing up!"

The Presents and Santa

It was amazing how fast we could get home from mass on Christmas morning. We all sat around the tree and were given presents in turn. Millions of families would be doing this around the world yet unfortunately for many others this happy time of giving and receiving would never take place.

About 10 o'clock, there was time out and we would rush outside to the sound of a bell, its toll getting louder and louder. Santa was on his way. He sat majestically in the back seat of a bright red Mk 1 Ford Zephyr Convertible. As he passed the houses, he would throw out little bags of lollies to the kids. I never knew who he was or to whom the car belonged. For years I was under the impression that this was Santa's mode of travel in spite of the pictures of Rudolph and Co. in the little story books.

The Chook Preparation

Once the opening of presents was over, and Santa had been and gone, Dad would march down to the chook house and haul out the mangiest and oldest non-egg laying chook. He would walk back towards the house and stop at the chopping block. He'd hold the chook by the feet upside down which seemed to hypnotise it, and gently lay it sideways on the block. With one whack with the axe, he'd lop its head off. We would all sit there in awe. This bloke knew how to do everything!

One year, he let the chook slip out of his hand and it raced across the lawn headless with Dad in hot pursuit. He needed to stop it before it ran under the house where it could not be retrieved. The prospect of a dead, rotting, stinking chook under the house for a week or two encouraged Dad to run one of his record-breaking sprints. Once he caught it he gutted it. At the same time he taught Kerry the finer points of chook gutting.

While they were gutting the chook Mum had been readying a large drum of boiling water for the next step. The chook was dropped into the hot water. Then Dad and Kerry started plucking the feathers. This was a grotty job as far as I was concerned. Boy did the feathers and the gut of the chook stink but I always watched to get a sight of the half dozen eggs inside the chook. They were all in different stages of development. This had always intrigued me.

It was now Mum's turn and she stuffed her favourite seasoning recipe into the chook and sewed up its bum. It then went into the baking dish and oven along with all sorts of vegetables to be roasted.

The Dinner

There were bound to be at least fifteen to twenty people arriving for dinner. When Auntie Roie brought her mob down from Woodstock, a farming district up the Motueka valley, the number swelled accordingly.

The guests consisted of our immediate family, various friends, and girlfriends and boyfriends during later years. There would also be a few locals Dad would invite from around the town. They had no family or so he thought, and would be quite alone for Christmas. For most people dinner was at noon but we were lucky to get started by 2.30 p.m. This was due to the long preparations and the time outs for the odd drink with visitors who would pop in and out throughout the morning.

The wait for dinner was worthwhile however and the range of food was as usual, quite incredible. All of it came from our own garden and chook house, except for the peas and the beer.

I will always remember those Christmas days and more specifically, our parents' generosity towards our guests, regardless of race, creed or colour.

Circus Bourke

Garry Bourke was a strange but likeable sort of a bloke. He was the same age as my brother Sean. Many people used to take the piss out of him. He was the sort of bloke you couldn't help but take the piss out of. How he got the nickname Circus, I will probably never know.

Garry's father used to manage the local bottle shop owned by the Manoy family. They retailed beer, wines and spirits.

I recall one of the Manoys being in the store now and again when I went there with Dad. I really don't know what the Manoys did the rest of the time. They had a big house with beautiful gardens on the northern outskirts of the town and Sean and I used to deliver their daily paper. At Christmas, Manoys gave us a huge tip for delivering the paper throughout the year. If I recall, the tip was a pound note! That was a lot of money.

About one o'clock one Saturday morning in 1965 or 1966, Garry was walking home from a party. As he got to the fire station on the main street, he could smell smoke. He walked around the back of the station and through a window, he saw the flames. The station, however, was locked up and there were no fire fighters on duty. Well there were, but they had been called out to a house fire about half an hour earlier and were a bit busy!

Mobile telephones had not been invented in those days. A public phone or any other phone would not work because the telephone exchange was closed for the night, as was the police station some fifty yards down the street. Everything seemed to close for the night in those days and pity help anyone if there was any sort of an emergency. There was a town siren that went off occasionally and we had to guess what the emergency was. Generally, a fire we supposed.

Garry sat down on the side of the road across the street and simply watched the fire station burn to the ground! No one else came by so he stood up, looked around, and wandered off home.

When Garry was about ten years old, my brother Sean used to bully the shit out of him. Sean's modus operandi was a bit over the top at times but quite effective. One afternoon Sean was delivering papers on his paper round. As he rode past Bourke's house Garry's little cocker spaniel raced out and bit Sean on the foot. Just as Sean was making a move on the dog with the intention of strangling it, Garry came running out of the house which was lucky for the dog. Sean turned his attention to Garry instead.

I was riding my bike along behind Sean and by this time, I was laughing my head off at Sean's predicament. At this point Sean had Garry in a headlock. His eyes were bulging out of his head, his face was red and mouth gasping for air. The little spaniel was yapping and snapping at Sean's feet and he was trying to kick it away.

Then Sean tells Garry that he is going to throw him over the fence if he doesn't call his dog a mongrel. At the time, I thought that Garry was being very loyal to his dog by not complying with the request. I soon found out that the real reason was that he was choking to death and couldn't utter a word! When he did finally get a word out it was too late for he was on his way, up and over the fence. It was a great throw by Sean and as Garry hurtled over the fence, I heard him say, "My dog's a mongrel," before he crashed down through the geraniums.

Every night from then on, Garry would be waiting behind the closed gate for the paper. The dog nowhere in sight. As Sean rode up he'd fire the paper from under his arm at Garry's head and Garry would be yelling, "My dog's a mongrel, my dog's a mongrel."

That's why Sean always made me collect the paper money from Mr Bourke every fourth Saturday.

Garry turned out to be a good bloke but unfortunately he passed away at a relatively young age.

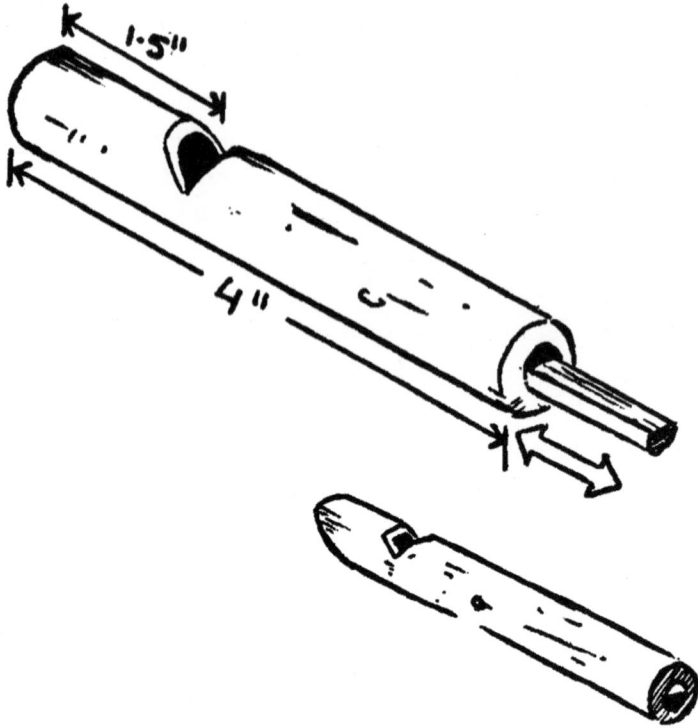

Willow Trees and Flax Arrows

The New Zealand flax bush and the English willow tree grew in abundance on the banks of the Motueka River. We never got round to making cricket bats from the willow wood but we certainly smoked the dried roots. We also made beaut little whistles from the pencil thin green branches. At the time, I was not aware that aspirin also came from willow trees. We probably would have had a shot at making that as well!

To make the whistle, cut a green willow branch about as thick as your forefinger and about four inches long. With the handle of a pocketknife, tap the green outer bark all the way around the piece and up and down its length. The outer layer or green bark can then be slipped off the inner white wood. Before sliding the outer off the inner, cut a V into the wood, through the green bark to about one-third the thickness of the wood. Make the V incision about one and a half inches from one end of the piece. Slide off the outer bark and cut a slice off the entire inner wood. Push the green outer back onto the inner making sure it is aligned to where it was originally. Blow into the whistle, keeping the V cut closest to your mouth.

A piccolo can be made in the same way by adding multiple V cuts along the length of the whistle. Take care to space the V cuts evenly.

The flax arrow can be a lot of fun. The flax leaves grow out from the base of the plant into five to six foot lengths. At the point where the leaves grow out from the plant's base, they are welded together by the sap but as the leaf progresses towards its tip, the leaf fans and flattens. In other words, the edges separate and part. Cut some of the leaves from the bush. Cut these to length to two and a half feet, measuring from the acute base end. Cut these into the shape of an arrow. *(Refer illustration)*

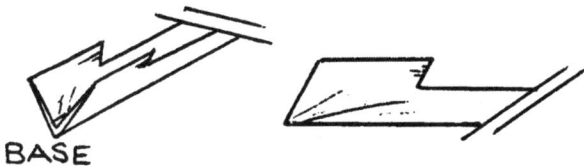

BASE

At the point "X", peel a three-inch strip from the base of the pointed end of the arrow, but leave it attached to the arrow.

Take some of the discarded flax leaf ends and tear into strips. Plait strips into a thin, strong rope about five feet long. Tie one end of the plaited flax rope to a length of straight willow branch, approximately four feet long.

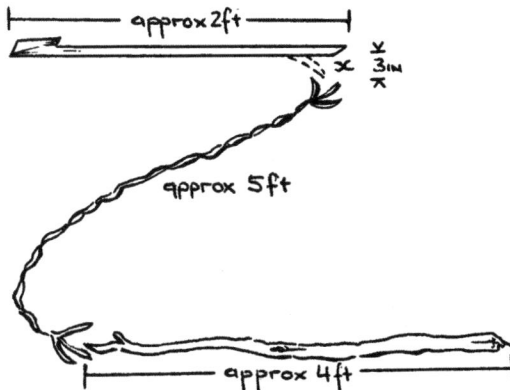

Tie the other end of the plaited flax rope to the peeled back strip on one of the arrows.

With the willow stick arced out behind you, slightly over your shoulder, take a short run and flick the stick forwards over your shoulder. As if you were bowling a cricket ball. The arrow will follow your arm action and when it reaches the apex of the arc the plaited rope extends to its fullest and the three-inch strip will tear off the bottom of the arrow. The arrow will continue in its headed direction. It should be flying out and upwards at about a forty-five degree angle and with practice, distances of well over one hundred yards can be achieved. Dad used to be able to flick flax arrows right out of the cricket ground, over the road, and beyond. His favourite landing place was on Mr Chang's roof. He was the local fruiterer. His was one of the few houses in the district with a flat roof and I recall Bevan Congdon, the New Zealand cricket captain at the time, hitting the odd cricket ball up on his roof as well.

Another use for the flax bush was for getting time off school to go whitebaiting. Dad was reluctant to tell us about this but he did in the end. When you cut a flax leaf from the bush and split the leaf down the centre, the end of the leaf emits a yellowish sticky liquid. Take some of this liquid and smear it on an arm or leg and wait a few minutes for it to dry. The result visually is not unlike a horrific scald or burn. This always tricked the nuns into sympathy and a couple of days off school during the whitebait season.

They must have wondered however, why it was only the Horgan kids that got these terrible burns. In hindsight I bet they wondered how in the hell we got them and what sort parental supervision went on at 29 Poole Street. You could let the "burn" linger for up to a week and let it wear off on its own accord. It faded away just like any normal graze or abrasion. Alternatively, you could simply wash it of with a good soapy scrub on Friday afternoon. You sure didn't want to be laid up for the weekend!

Whitebait

We didn't have a car but from time to time Dad used to look after friends' cars when they were away for long periods. Then one day in 1958 Dad bought a 1929 Chrysler. The car was his pride and joy and was the main mode of transport that took us down to the river whitebaiting.

We were at the age where most of our time was spent at school, or during the months of August through November, down on the banks of the Motueka River, near the mouth. The reason was that this was the season for whitebait fishing.

Whitebait are tiny, almost transparent fish, the size of matchsticks. They have two black eyes, the size of pinpricks. They hatch in the rivers and migrate to the ocean. In spring and early summer they return to the rivers to spawn, and complete the cycle. They turn white within a short time after taking them from the rivers.

Other countries such as China, Chile, Australia and England also claim to have fish called whitebait but these are quite different species and not as transparent as the New Zealand ones. The New Zealand whitebait, or Inanga, consists of five or six different species but the difference is not great.

When Dad was a younger man in his late thirties, I remember him and his old mate, Bill Hodgetts, who was an Australian Aboriginal, catching over a hundred pounds of whitebait in a single day. They could not give it away and used to spread it under fruit trees as manure.

The largest recorded catch in the Waimakariri River in Canterbury was 240 pounds in one day, in 1925. The largest recorded catch in the Wataroa River, on the West Coast was in 1928. This was just over 1,100 pounds. There may well have been larger catches in intervening years but these were never recorded. According to records, the period between 1955 and 1957 seems to have been the best for whitebaiting during the last 80 years. In 2007 however, there were some huge catches on the West Coast of the South Island. Catches of 1000 pounds and 1600 pounds on a single tide were reported. This supports a theory I have regarding the so-called declining catches. I totally disagree with the experts and believe that there is a fifty to sixty year cycle. (I explain this at the end of this chapter.)

There was no refrigeration until the mid to late '50s and canneries were set up on the west coast of the South Island to can the fish. It was then transported to the cities for sale. The canneries closed in the late 1950s and refrigeration replaced them.

By the late fifties and early sixties, whitebait had become scarce. Seasons were shortened and many other restrictions were introduced. There are many theories as to why the fish became scarce, but no one has conclusive proof as to the decline. In the late seventies in the Motueka River, a catch of five pounds of whitebait was not considered exceptional, but now in 2008, a five pound catch by the average white baiter on a single tide is not that common.

As a schoolboy in the sixties, I used to sell whitebait in the town for ten bob or ten shillings a pound. (One dollar in today's currency.) In 2008, the price is sometimes in excess of sixty dollars a pound.

On the other hand, there are professional whitebaiters, on the West Coast of the South Island, who may catch as much as five or six thousand pounds or more, in a season. However, I have never been whitebaiting on the West Coast of New Zealand and am not qualified to write about it. What I do know is that any reporter or writer who ventures to the West Coast in search of an in-depth story will do so in vain. The professional whitebaiters down there are very secretive about their catches and fair enough, it is their livelihood.

A friend of mine, George, who lives in Motueka but was born in the town of Westport on the West Coast, tells of the story when he was about six years old. His father and he went fishing on the first day of the season at the mouth of the Buller River. George's job on that first day was to take the first shoal of whitebait caught and cook it up, immediately, on the bank of the river. His father was fishing in front of him. George had a kid sized net. As the tide started to come in George's father spotted an enormous shoal of whitebait entering his net. The shoal was so large that it just kept coming and coming. In the end, George's father attempted to lift the net out of the water because it was full. As he lifted the net, the whole thing fell apart with the sheer weight of the fish and George's father fell into the river after it! George reckons to this day that he saved his father's life by hauling him out of the river with the handle of his kid's net, but that was not enough. His father raced upstream, soaking wet, armed with George's little net and tried to catch some of the shoal that had caused the problem in the first place.

To us and to most of the whitebaiters in Motueka, whitebaiting is fun, and this is what takes us back each year. It is almost an addiction. To others, it is about as interesting as watching the grass grow. I am thankful for that, as it keeps the hordes away from the river. Most of the whitebait we catch is given away to friends and to the old folk in the town. Those who used to be keen whitebaiters and who can no longer go down to the river to catch their own. It is quite a thrill to turn up at their homes with a fresh catch of whitebait. I guess payback for the times we were little tearaways around their neighbourhood!

Whitebait is a delicacy in New Zealand. It is by far the highest rated and priced fish. It has a unique flavour and yet not everyone likes it. It can be cooked in many different ways, the most common being in the form of a whitebait omelette with a touch of lemon.

Many of my childhood memories are based on our adventures down the Motueka River whitebaiting.

Whitebaiters have favourite positions or "possies" on the riverbank from which they fish. They are notorious for their secrecy, skulduggery, and for getting up early in the morning to secure their possie. Some even sleep on the riverbank overnight to ensure they get what they think is the best spot on the river to fish.

There are rules and regulations for whitebait fishing such as size of nets and screens, distance between nets, staying with your net at all times, etc, but there is no limit on the daily size of catch.

Whitebaiters also have little cartels, unwritten, unspoken, but there nonetheless. These are small groups of people who fish a selected area and who are wary of strangers. Strangers are those from other towns who now and then, arrive at the river and pinch a local whitebaiter's possie. There is no law against this but it is frowned upon by some. It is OK however, for a local to pinch a local's possie, with the odd exception! There will always be the odd asshole or bully who will issue the odd threat, if someone takes his possie.

There are also unwritten rules such as only heathens or morons walk close to the riverbank in front, or immediately behind, someone else's net. Yet if it is someone from your own cartel, then it is OK because you know that you can trust him or her not to scare the fish away.

Strangers to the area are sometimes considered novices, but in fact, they may be better at the game than you are. Whitebaiters rarely tell anyone how much they have caught. When asked, answers are "a few" or "a cup full." Other answers are "a cold", or "I strained a hell of a lot of water today for nothing."

Summing it up: "that whitebaiters are somewhat paranoid" is an understatement!

There are many types of nets, from muslin scoop nets to set nets made from a steel frame wrapped in fine wire mesh, similar to insect screens. Set nets are generally made from a frame of quarter inch galvanized steel rod, welded into a rectangular shape, a bit like a small hockey net. The netting is wrapped around all sides and one end. The other end is open and the net is placed in the river, close to the riverbank, with the open end facing the sea. Whitebait enter the rivers and the ones hugging the riverbanks are the target, and hopefully swim into the net.

Most whitebaiters use cream or white coloured "spotters" which are lengths of colourbond steel, approximately six feet long and six inches wide. These are placed in the river, on the riverbed, at intervals in front of the net. The fish are easier to see as they pass over the spotters. A hole in the bottom of a net the circumference of a ballpoint pen will let a fair sized shoal escape before you can lift the net out of the water.

Whitebaiters need good eyesight and a hell of a lot of patience. It takes a novice a while to be able to spot whitebait in the river. Eventually your eyes train to focus on them and from then on, it is reasonably easy to spot them. This is only when the water is clear and there is little or no wind. Their being almost transparent does not help. They can be very timid and seem to have good eyesight. Whitebaiters need to stand very still on the riverbank or the shoals of fish will veer out into deeper water, away from the net. A slight hand movement or shadow will also scare them.

These tiny fish can swim extremely fast up the rivers as single fish or in shoals of millions. I have seen shoals of five or six pound but down on the West Coast, I understand they can be ten times that big. Large shoals swim majestically. They resemble a travelling mist in the water. They can maintain a speed faster than a man's walking speed, and can do this against a good current. Sometimes they will dawdle along, and even back track. In this mode, they are very flighty. Some days they swim high in the water and other days they swim low and there is no predicting what they will do on a given day.

Whitebait generally swim or run upstream on the incoming tide, but they have been known to run at any time of the day. In other words, when they run, they run, regardless of time, tide, or water colour. No one has been able to figure out their fickle nature.

There is more than a theory, that whitebait will mass in their millions or in hundreds of pounds a few hundred metres from the breaker line out from the river mouth. They will wait there for some sort of signal, whether it is temperature, a certain time or tide, or other sign of nature. Then as one, they will make a run for the river mouth.

Many years ago, I was in a fishing boat off the coast in Golden Bay, fishing for schnapper. As we neared the mouth of one of the rivers, we anchored and prepared our lines. In the sea directly beneath the boat, whitebait were everywhere. Just one huge mass, not unlike a giant grey submarine, waiting to attack the river-mouth. I know of others who have seen this in the bay.

The next day I couldn't wait to get down to the river, expecting to catch whitebait by the bucket full. I caught none. Moreover, I caught none every day for the next week. Where they had gone I would never know. I made phone calls to friends who had been fishing the other rivers in the bay on the same days and they had seen no sign of a large run of white bait. In fact, the season passed without reports of any catches out of the ordinary.

As a young boy I remember Mum and Dad coming home from a Friday night party next door. They were laughingly quoting the neighbour, Jack Crisp, saying, "The whitebait are running, you can hear them coming!" A slight exaggeration I guess, but there is such a thing as whitebait fever!

If only we knew the trigger or signal from nature that sends these tiny fish into the rivers to spawn. There are river mouths dotted along the shores of Tasman Bay at various intervals. Whitebait will run in some rivers one day, others the next and in some rivers not at all.

Some say it is the phase of the moon, others say that's rubbish! There has to be a trigger and the trigger is probably a simple one. My personal belief is that the trigger is a combination of all the right conditions occurring simultaneously. Sun, moon, tide, watercolour, temperature, wind, rain, etc. A combination of all the elements.

This total combination of the right elements may only occur once every fifty years, or even longer, and it may occur for two or three seasons in a row. Much like the red tides or the locust plagues of Africa — when the elements are in harmony, they multiply to plague proportions.

Short of inventing a "whitebait cam", we may never solve the riddle and it is probably just as well because if we did, we would probably well and truly see the whitebait's total demise!

The Hut Down The River

When standing at our back gate looking into the park, off to the right at about two o'clock, there was a corrugated iron shed. It had an easily pickable, lockable steel door, a corrugated iron roof and sat on a concrete slab. The shed housed the motor mowers for the cricket pitch and the park. The mowers' petrol tanks were often peed in by small boys. The shed also had a lean-to attached to it, which sheltered the cricket pitch roller. We never had a use for the roller so it stayed there relatively unscathed.

Before he bought the "Yank Tank", his much loved 1929 Chrysler, most mornings Dad would walk to work. He took the short cut via the gate in the fence at the bottom of our yard. He'd cross the cricket ground with the mower shed, pass the war memorial and Post Office Hotel and enter the Post Office, a distance of about three hundred yards. He would walk home for lunch, then back to work and finally, after a detour into the hotel, walk the same way home.

Early one morning, before school and before Dad went to work, my brother Sean, who was thirteen at the time, asked Dad if he would borrow a car and trailer from someone. "The object," Sean said, "was to take some bits of wood and tin down to the river." He'd planned to build a hut for the coming whitebait season.

Dad was good like that and sure enough, he came home from work with a borrowed car and trailer. We loaded up Sean's "bits of wood and tin" and trundled off with the load to the river. Over the next week or so, Sean, Kerry and I proceeded to build the hut. It turned out perfect, and so it should have.

At tea time, about a week after we took Sean's "bits of wood and tin" down to the river, Dad looked up from his meal at Mum and said, "Jan, you would not believe it. You know the mower shed out in the cricket ground?" Mum nodded her head. "Well it's gone. Silly bloody council," he said. "Fancy them taking down the shed and leaving the motor mowers sitting out there on a slab of concrete in the rain." Sean kept on eating and I was trying not to cry. He was kicking me under the table, trying to induce a bawling session to change the topic of conversation.

What Sean had done was to number every sheet of iron and every piece of timber on the mower shed and dismantle it. It was this very same timber and corrugated iron that Dad had carted down the river for him a few days before!

Sean and I suspected that Dad knew about the conversion all along. He wanted to let us know that he knew, and that it was not really the right thing for Sean to do. Dad could never reprimand us for it in front of Mum or the grit would have really hit the fan. She had no sense of humour for that sort of thing.

Some weeks later, during the whitebait season, Dad, Sean, Kerry and I were down the river by the hut. Dad was inspecting the re-build out of the corner of his eye and said, "Your Uncle Allan, who is one of the District Cricket Selectors, was wondering if I knew anything about the missing mower shed!" With that, he smiled and walked away, whittling on a willow stick, probably thinking up a story for his brother-in-law.

The Great Fire

The Motueka River separates two districts, Motueka and Riwaka. From a whitebaiting point of view, the river has a "Mot side" and a "Riwaka side." The side you live on is the side you should fish on. It is an unwritten law!

My first visit down there was when I was four years old. I can still recall the smell of the willows, gorse, and wattle in flower at the start of the whitebait season. Sean built a hut that was a masterpiece as far as huts down the river go. Even today in 2008, we fish on the same spot, just along from where Sean's hut used to be. We have fished there each year for over fifty years although the river has altered somewhat over that time. There were only two other huts on the Motueka side of the river. A bloke called Hongi Hamilton had built one many years before. The other was built and owned by a bloke called Jack Brodie.

Hongi actually lived in Riwaka but his hut was on the Motueka side, right on Hongi's point, and only the last bit made sense I guess. I often wondered why Hongi fished on the Mot side. His sons fished there as well.

He actually lived in the hut for the whole three months of the season. Maybe the people of Riwaka had banned him from their side of the river for some reason. Maybe he just needed to get away from a nagging wife – who knows!

Then there were two old hermits, Jack Brodie and Joe Hardacre. They were legends on the river. Jack had built his hut and lived on the river full time, all year round. Then the great flood in 1956 washed his hut and all his worldly possessions out into Tasman Bay. Jack vanished from the river as well and I often wondered if he too went with the flood. Probably did because I never saw him after that. Joe Hardacre lived in a large tent complete with a fly. He also lived on the river all year round. It was difficult to get near either of these two old blokes simply because of the stink.

Jack Brodie was really weird, and pretty scary, but Joe wasn't a bad old bloke once you got to know him. They both fished their fiercely guarded positions for every tide of the season and probably before the season as well. Anyone who dare pinch their possie or set up a net within fifty yards of them had better look out.

Dad was the only bloke who could walk anywhere near where they were fishing without being howled down upon. He would walk along the stones on the edge of the river casting his rod for trout. He'd be walking along, whistling away, casting his minnow out into the river, stopping, and then winding it in. Every few yards he would repeat the process. He would deliberately walk right in front of their nets, whistling away without a care in the world. I didn't see him do it the first time and often wondered what had been the reaction from Jack and Joe. I think the reason that Dad got away with it was that he was the man at the Post Office who looked after pension payments and banking. He handled Jack and Joe's transactions and was someone they could trust. I only guessed this of course.

Jack and Joe had one thing in common, and that was that they could, and did, catch a hell of a lot of whitebait. Maybe the stink attracted them.

Anyway, on with the story. It was about 1959 or 1960 at the start of the August school holidays. The season got off to a hiss and a roar with some pretty good catches recorded.

It was Friday afternoon on the eve of the first day of the holidays. Lots of boys from the local high school and some from their last years in primary school were heading down to the river. They biked down there loaded up with all sorts of gear, intending to spend a couple of fun days away from home. They had tents, sleeping bags, carbide and kerosene lamps, camp stoves, nets, flour, milk, eggs and cooking utensils. Each one intent on catching heaps of whitebait and cooking it up on the riverbank.

A tent city sprang up just above the high water mark on the riverbank at the junction where Moon Creek joined the Motueka River. My brother Sean's hut was about one hundred yards back upstream from tent city. Some of the older boys had bottles of warm beer and as twilight closed into darkness, campfires sprang up outside most of the tents. After a while, kids were tearing around with blankets over their heads and lighted sticks with dry gorse wrapped around the ends. Sort of like a junior Ku Klux Klan rally.

The night wore on and about 8.30 p.m. there was a little non-camp fire like glow from somewhere within tent city. How the tent caught fire, no one knew. It could possibly have been a spark from a campfire but whatever the cause, the result was to become quite spectacular. Soon after the tent, a couple of dry gorse bushes caught fire. Then a small group of boys whose tent was the first to catch fire deliberately set another tent alight. They thought that the boys next to them had set their tent on fire. On it went until everyone's tent was on fire.

One would have thought that with all this water about — the river is two hundred yards wide and reasonably deep — any fire could be quickly extinguished. However, there were no buckets or containers handy. The few buckets that could have been used were mangled or melted in the fires. The remaining containers had holes in the bottom and they were used as whitebait strainers. You tip whitebait from the net into buckets or strainers. The holes in the strainers drain any excess water and the whitebait are then tipped into plastic bags. If you did not have a bucket with tiny holes in the bottom, you would probably have had a wooden box with fine wire mesh nailed to the bottom called a strainer, and this served the same purpose.

The whole kit and caboodle burned to a cinder. Twenty or thirty tents, sleeping bags, food, whitebait nets that bent, buckled and melted, along with some of the kids' bikes. Luckily, no one was hurt or burnt.

After about an hour of kids wandering about in the eerie glow of the fire's embers and the smoke haze, a light shower of rain hit what was left of tent city. This produced a hissing and fizzing noise from the half-burnt twigs and branches which were still smouldering. A cloud of steam and smoke rose, forming an almost un-breathable mist for about a square mile around tent city. It hung like a dense grey fog, just a few feet off the ground.

About 10.30 p.m., the kids realised that they would be better off at home. One by one, and then in small groups, they collected what was left of their belongings and started the long trek home. The rain had stopped, a breeze blew up, and the string of miserable, wet and grumpy kids made their way upstream along the track on the river bank. They passed the neat, corrugated iron hut of a supposedly sleeping trio of Horgan brothers. A couple of the brighter kids were heard to mumble that the "shed" looked familiar. They hurled a few rocks onto the roof of the hut and on they trekked.

From within the hut, six small eyes stared through old nail holes, mouths and noses not daring to breathe or make a sound as the miserable mob trudged past. The three small suspects would have the pick of the whitebaiting positions in the morning as soon as the sun rose and they had large smiles on their small faces.

Some fifty years later, there are some prominent businessmen in the town of Motueka, who will still remember that night. They may either laugh or cry, yet few will ever find out the real cause of the fire!

Kerry and I often wondered why there was no kerosene in the can used for lighting the lamp and the camp stove the next morning. We dared not ask our older brother why he had snuck out in the darkness the night before. Nor did we ask why he was laughing when he came back an hour later.

Sean's hut vanished in a flood a couple of years later but it had served its purpose. A new concrete block mower shed was built in the park behind the houses in Poole Street. I'm sure my Uncle Allan would have been pleased about that.

Carbide

As you walked down our garden path you came to a gate in a high hawthorn fence that in turn led out into Memorial Park. It was simply known, however, as the cricket ground because that was its main use.

A wonderful grassed oval and playground for eight lucky families. They were fortunate enough to live on our side of the street, and all had private access to the park. As you walked through the gate, to your left and right were some magnificent trees. These were a mix of silver birch, black beech, oregon, maple, fir and oak. They would have been planted about 1900 or before. Across to your right on the edge of the park was a men's dunny. It was a corrugated iron shed built in the form of a maze with no roof. The concrete floor had a moulded hollow around three sides where the men stood and peed and the pee eventually disappeared through a hole in the corner of the shed. I never knew where it went from there. The dunny stank!

Years ago, when we went fishing for flounder we would use a net or a spear. Fishing with a spear, or gaf, was generally done at night in the pools on the mud flats when the tide was coming in. To see the flounder, we used a carbide lamp. This type of lamp gives off a very powerful white light. It enables you to see the outline of the flounder on the sandy bottom of the water, which is from twelve to twenty four inches deep. We'd then spear them, making allowance for the distortion, being careful not to spear the odd foot!

You may be wondering where this story is going but carbide had two uses for kids in Motueka. Carbide's raw form is like small irregularly shaped pebbles or like the modern day blue metal stone road base. It is approximately one inch cubed. A carbide lamp has a compartment into which you put the dry carbide pebbles and then add a small amount of water. The mixture gives off a gas, which is ignited at a point in front of the lamp's reflector. It is much like a car headlight but twice the size with a lot more candle power.

The second use for carbide was for our little acts of terrorism. Petrol based Molotov cocktails are firecrackers in comparison to a carbide cocktail. The dunny in the park was our testing ground for such weapons or our equivalent of the South Australian nuclear testing ground of Maralinga. We would take a large beer or lemonade bottle; add water, just a thimble full, and drop in a few chips of carbide. Then we'd jam the top back on the bottle and roll it round the door of the maze shaped dunny. You had to be reasonably quick during the process as you can imagine or you wouldn't be around to do it a second time.

As the gas builds, the bottle shatters into millions of bits of glass, some of them sliver shaped. You could add the odd nail or staple if you wished, depending on the target! We'd lie outside the dunny flat on the grass or behind a tree and within a few seconds there would be a deafening and shattering explosion. The noise of the glass particles and shards hitting the walls of the dunny was incredible. The echo almost burst our eardrums.

If thirty blokes were standing in the dunny taking a piss at the time you would probably get the lot. The explosion was so vicious that some of the glass particles would penetrate right through the corrugated iron walls of the dunny. After a while, the dunny walls looked like a colander. The lingering stench of the carbide, however, sure disguised the dunny stink.

The other trick with carbide was to take a screw top jar, place a few drops of water in it, add the carbide, and screw on the top in a hurry. This would take place down the river and once the lid was screwed on we would drop the jar in the water upstream from a water hole where we thought trout were lurking. We would lie flat on the river bank while the jar floated over the waterhole. When the jar exploded we would race over to the river and scoop out the stunned trout and eels!

There were hazards of carbide bombs however. One was the stink of the stuff. Another was the limited amount of time we had to dispose of the bomb after we had put the lid on the bottle.

That you can no longer buy carbide is a positive thing.

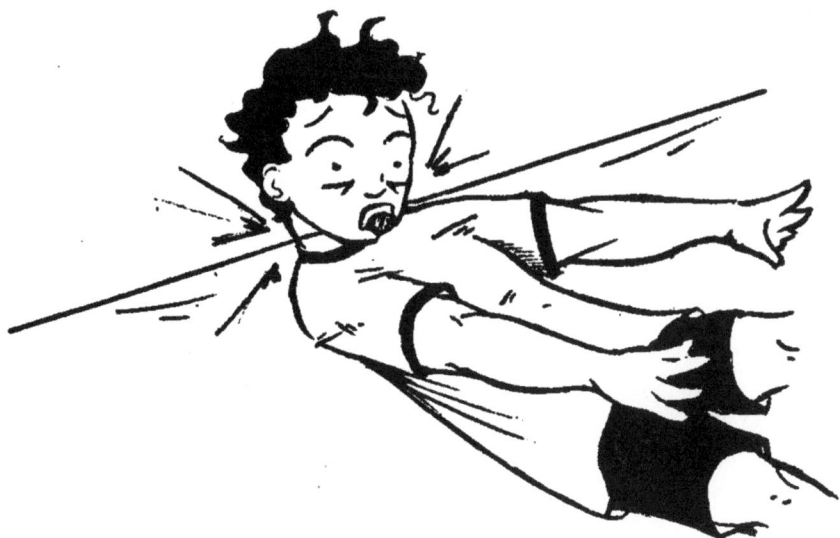

The Bike Race

My brother Sean and I had this thing about pushbikes. Not so much as riding them but building and modifying them.

Sean had just finished his last year of primary school and was off to high school at the end of January. One of his mates, Michael Stebbings, came over to our place to show off the brand new green and white sports bike he had received for his birthday.

The closest we ever got to brand new bikes were very second hand ones or bitsers. Bitsers were bikes made up of parts from all makes and models. My brother Kerry got a new bike when he finally recovered from an ongoing, stunt your growth, illness. Ongoing meaning he was sick for about a year. What some kids would do for a new bike is amazing.

Anyway, Sean reckoned that one of his home built bikes would beat

Michael's new bike in a race from our back door to the gate down at the bottom of the garden. The gate led out into the cricket ground. It was a distance of about seventy-five yards. My job was to hold the gate open and judge the winner.

The concrete garden path to the back gate was barely wide enough for one bike, let alone two abreast. The path ended in grass about five yards before the gate. This made it a bit less obvious that the path didn't actually line up with the gate, which was offset to the right a bit.

On the right hand side where the concrete path ended, there was a post in the garden. There was another post further out to the right on the fence line where there was an apple tree. Between these posts were two wires running from post to post, one at ground level and the other at the five-foot mark. This year Dad had "not yet" run the strings from the bottom wire to the top to allow the beans that he had also "not yet" planted, to climb up.

Mum, however, had recently planted some of her best gladioli corms from a range of 10,000 varieties. Her glads were obviously a substitute for the beans this year. Their shoots had just broken through the ground and were about three inches high. These were the glads for the first of the flower shows in late January and early February. She had already started nurturing them with heaps of tender loving care. There were three rows, stretching from the pathway to the fence.

Michael, on the right hand side of the pathway, was winning the race by about a wheel and a half and was about ten yards from the end of the path. Standing at the gate, I saw he had the race won. Then Sean put on a quick spurt to be neck and neck. For some crazy reason Michael thought he could gain a yard by cutting off the path via the garden on a more direct route to the gate. He hadn't seen the wire at the five foot mark and never actually made the gate but his new bike did.

Sean flew through the gate at the same time as Michael's bike bounced off the apple tree, the front wheel now square. The bike then flew past me and followed Sean through the gate cart wheeling end over end.

Michael had been waylaid a bit! While his bike was cart wheeling through the gate, he was doing three or four loops around the wire at the five-foot mark of the bean fence, the wire under his chin. Prior to the wire, Michael had a pronounced Adam's apple, which was quite rare for a young kid. He didn't have it any more.

Mum had extra sensory perception when it came to gladioli, especially when they were hers. Even more so if they were her prized corms as she called them. She could almost "sense" people thinking bad things about her bloody glads. Michael had sheared a couple of shoots off them. He was now in very deep shit, not from the wire, his neck, the buggered new bike, his old man when he got home, or from his now non-existent Adam's apple. His immediate problem was Mrs Horgan's coal pan.

Mum had been out at the coal bin getting a couple of shovels full of coal for the incinerator. Now here she was, on the scene as quick as a flash, whacking the crap out of Michael's head, arms, bum and legs with a few "lucky for Michael" air shots. He could hardly breathe and was croaking out, "I could have killed myself." Mum was yelling back, "Don't worry, I'm going to do that anyway."

Michael's Catherine Wheel ride around the wire had left some awful red welts across his neck. Mum must have now seen them and stopped trying to kill him with the coal pan. I doubted very much if she was about to give him mouth to mouth or an "Are you OK?" Instead, she checked out the two broken glad shoots. Then she stormed off to her corm shed to hunt for some new corms to re-plant in the hope they would grow and be ready in time for the first flower show.

Michael lost his voice for about a month and never stopped by to see us for a while, especially if Mrs Horgan was home!

Rolley's 1100 and The Chook House

The local parish priest came to Motueka in 1957 from a small town in the North Island of New Zealand called Opunake, in the province of Taranaki. Taranaki boasts a volcano, some great ex All Blacks such as Ross Brown and Neil Wolfe and some green grass with lots of cows. There is also a bit of oil off-shore and that's about all.

Not long after the priest arrived in Motueka, and built a new presbytery, a middle-aged lady called Mrs Bowler followed. Most people called her Rolley except me. She became the priest's housekeeper. It was no wonder he conned her into coming to Motueka. She was wealthy, a really kind and lovely person and a great cook. She smoked like a chimney and so did the priest.

She brought her car with her, a Morris Minor 1000. She had bought it new in 1958 and it was now 1961. So she decided to trade it in for a new model, the Morris 1100. I was eleven years old.

You couldn't just go out and buy a new car in those days. You had to have what were called overseas funds and you had to sacrifice some of those mysterious funds as payment for a new car. Many people bought new cars and I often wondered how they got their overseas funds. I honestly thought that there was some sort of a racket going on. How did the local priest get a brand new 1963 American Ford Fairlane and before that a 1956 American Dodge Desoto? I seriously doubted if he would have had overseas funds.

The theory was that no matter how much money you had in New Zealand you could not buy a new car unless you had those mysterious overseas funds. My theory was that you went to the car dealer who did have the overseas funds. He transferred the required amount into your name overseas, took his cut and whammo, you had a new car. Something along those lines, I am sure was happening. Whatever the trick was, it was obvious that bankers and car dealers knew how to get around it.

The new 1100 duly arrived. It was a shit brown colour and had a four-speed manual gearshift. Automatic gearboxes were only just arriving on the scene. Many of the men around the town swore black and blue on manual gearboxes and reckoned that automatics would never replace them. They also insisted that automatic gear changing was a sign that there would be a sharp increase in road deaths. Their reckoning was that more people would drift off to sleep while driving, as they had nothing to do. Just as well car manufacturers did not also try to introduce cruise control.

About the same time, dealers started importing Japanese cars. In many cases, people boycotted them. Some because of what the Japs did during the war. Some because there was an illusion that the Jap cars were rust buckets, were flimsy, and for some other oddball reasons.

A family friend bought a new Datsun Bluebird. It was a great little car and it long out-ran his previous UK built Humber 80. I know because my brother Sean bought the Humber. Then again, Sean thrashed the guts out of it so I suppose one could not make an accurate assessment of car versus car longevity using the "Sean factor."

The Catholic school was built in a corner site on about six acres of land. In addition to the new presbytery, a full sized rugby field was marked out on the site. Mini market gardens within the boundary bordered both sides of the football field. Except for a gorse hedge, there were no fences down the sides of the property. The hedge was overgrown and totally out of control. However, it was probably better than any sort of conventional fence from a security point of view as gorse is a very prickly, almost impenetrable, English bush.

Down the end of the property about a hundred and fifty yards from the presbytery, was a sort of a swamp, which now and then produced thousands of tadpoles then thousands of frogs. It was down here that my brother Kerry and the priest decided to build a chook house. "Why buy eggs when you could grow your own?" they argued.

The chook project was one of many these two embarked upon. Others included growing a couple of acres of runner beans and buying fancy, but absolutely useless prototype ride-on and push mowers, from the local hardware store. The hardware store owner always "saw them coming". When the fancy mower thing wore off, they decided a goat would be a better option. It worked for a few months but the goat kept growing and growing and ended up like a balloon. One day it simply exploded. It had some sort of a pooping problem and nobody had noticed.

Before that though, they built the chook shed but let the chooks roam free all day. They locked the chooks up at night and then wondered why there were never any eggs. It wasn't until they ripped down one of the gorse hedges that they found hundreds of eggs in nests under the gorse bushes. A fenced yard was then hurriedly built for the chooks. They also installed externally opening nesting and feeding boxes for easy access. "The Hilton Chook House".

The chook fad soon passed and they then got into making cane baskets with a view to selling them. They should have just bought a couple of container loads from Fiji! Anyway, the responsibility of looking after the chooks was left to Mrs Bowler. The job then passed on to me.

Mrs Bowler and I had a wet days only "drive down to chooks agreement". Usually I would cart the chook food down the footy field on my bike or on the ride-on mower. On wet days we agreed that I could load up the new Morris 1100 with the food and water and drive it down to the chooks. The chook's evening meal consisted of hot mash, spud skins, wheat and water.

I prayed for many rainy days. It was not often an eleven year old kid would get to drive a new Morris 1100. After a few wet days Mrs Bowler didn't bother to come down to the chooks with me. Not only that, after a month or so I got to feed the chooks every day via the Morris 1100, regardless of the weather. On dry days, I could get the Morris 1100 up to fifty-five miles an hour at the point of the twenty-five yard mark at the far end of the football field. Sometimes I fed the chooks four times a day just to further hone my driving skills.

One wet afternoon I took off to feed the chooks. I had a couple of buckets of water, one of hot mash and spud skins and one of wheat, on the floor of the car. I had the priest's dog Rastus in the passenger's seat. Normally I wouldn't race the car on the outward journey because of the buckets of water. I would do it on the way back and the odd broken egg wouldn't hurt because Rastus loved eggs, but this day I was in a bit of a hurry.

Wet grass, dry grass was all the same to me in those days as far as cars and speed went. Even though it was wet, I had managed to get the 1100 up to fifty miles an hour by the time I reached the half way mark on the football field. I got to the twenty-five yard line and hadn't spilt much water, before making my customary little three hundred and sixty degree spin on the grass. I turned the wheel and pulled on the hand brake and nothing happened. The car kept going straight ahead and even the foot brake made no difference. I'd not experienced this before and the chook house was looming large! It was coming at me at fifty miles an hour.

It hit in the centre of the 1100's grill and the impact point on the chook house was on the right hand front corner. Splintered wood, corrugated iron, wire netting, feathers and chook shit flew through the air. Water, wheat, mash and spud skins were awash in what was left of the car. The windscreen and side windows were broken, the roof buckled and the radiator and bonnet were buggered. Steam and smoke poured out of the car and any chooks still alive were bolting for the swamp.

The car had a seatbelt, which was unusual for that era and for some reason I had been wearing it. Just like Stirling Moss! I made a dazed and sorry walk in the rain back to the presbytery. Along the way, trying to think up an excuse such as, "The brakes failed". Well they did in a way!

I told Mrs Bowler that the car was still down at the chook house and that it wouldn't start. Probably had water in the carburettor or something, "… among other things," I mumbled. I then made an excuse to ride home on my bike before it got dark, as my light was not working. Just like the lights on the 1100 at the moment, I thought.

At about 6.30 that night, we had a visit from the local priest. Dad was in for it this time! However, that was nothing new. He could handle it on his own I thought. I put my raincoat on, jumped out of the bedroom window and took off down to Grandma's and my mate Lummy's house to watch the Monkees on TV.

They found Rastus the next day cowering in the rubble of the chook house. He must have gone through the windscreen on impact. He survived but would never ride in a car again. He developed a hatred for chooks and a hatred for me for the rest of his life. Just as well he only had a couple of teeth. I silently congratulated my brother Kerry for that fact.

Kerry used to throw fried bacon rinds to Rastus from the back door of the presbytery's kitchen. Mrs Bowler would cook the priest bacon and eggs and cut off the rinds. As each rind was thrown, Rastus would leap up and catch it in his mouth with a "crunch and swallow" action. Every now and then, Kerry would throw a teaspoon! Rastus never learned.

Puddles

Much has been written about New Zealand's whitebait. Very little however, has been written about the preparation for, and the actual trip to the river and to the preferred fishing spot of prospective whitebaiters.

It can be quite a challenge and it most certainly was during the 1950s if you wanted to fish on the south eastern riverbank of the Motueka River.

Even though the best fishing spots were barely a mile or so from the main road, those last few hundred yards could be a minefield. It was a journey in the dark for only the foolish and the brave.

In hindsight, all the effort to try and catch a few tiny transparent fish, was for most people, a huge waste of time and effort.

But still they went to the river on those cold and sometimes very wet and windy *mornings.*

For some inexplicable reason both boys and men love to ride their pushbikes through puddles of water. They tear down the street and in the distance spot a puddle. Without giving it a second thought, they make a beeline for the puddle and as they near it they lift their feet and legs high off the pedals. They hit it with great speed. Water sprays everywhere. It is quite silly actually.

I guess it is a boy thing really, developed in those early years. The sheer joy of seeing the wave of water spraying out each side of the front wheel. To see it splashing pedestrians on the footpath, and giving the boy a quick getaway on the bike. As the boy grows, his mind stays young and puddle riding stays as a thrill in his bicycle repertoire. But the adult now usually performs the trick when he thinks no one else is looking.

Every year during the whitebait season males of every age, and some hardy females, make their way to the vicinity of the mouth of the Motueka River to fish. In the 1950s if you wanted to fish on the Motueka side of the river, you had to walk the last two miles or ride a bike through cow and sheep paddocks dotted with willow trees and patches of prickly gorse bushes. There was no road for a car. Very few people had cars anyway and if they did, they could afford to buy their whitebait as opposed to fishing for it.

At the start of the season the pedestrians and bike riders would follow the worn and winding sheep tracks through the long grass and cow patties. The tracks meandered along heading for the river. These tracks were no more than eight inches wide and sometimes so deep that you had to be careful that the bike's pedals did not hit the sides of the indented tracks.

Regardless of when the tide was due, most whitebaiters went down to the river in the early hours of the morning. This was to secure the best possible fishing position on the bank of the river. If the tide was not due until the mid-afternoon, it was a long and lonely wait.

You had your backpack, probably a net with a long handle protruding out over the handlebars, and all sorts of other gear. This consisted of thigh gumboots, torch, thermos flask of hot water, food, and little glass containers of sugar, tea and milk. There would be a strainer for the whitebait, or a bucket, perhaps a folding stool and matches for smokes and a fire. Dunny paper, and other bits and pieces, most of which were unnecessary were taken just in case.

Unless there was a full moon and no cloud cover, it was as dark and as cold as ice in those early mornings. It often rained. Therefore, you would be dressed in several layers of clothing with a beanie on your head and an oilskin raincoat over the lot.

"The raincoat caught in the chain thing" was all you needed at that hour in the morning. Especially when you were carrying all your gear, precariously packed on your person and your bike. It was quite a juggling act to do this while riding down the street, let alone on a meandering sheep track in the dark.

Once the flapping coat tail caught in between the bike's chain and the sprocket there was no escape! Something had to give. The coat would normally be zipped and buttoned up to your neck. The rain hood was stitched to the collar of the coat and oilskin coats were tough.

You felt the coat stiffen and start to tighten around your upper body. You could not back pedal to free the coat, as that would only gobble up more of the oilskin. The net was over your shoulder, held in your right hand by its handle and your left hand was the only contact with the bike for steering purposes.

The front handbrake was on the left side of the handlebars. If you applied it, because of the top heaviness of the bike, you and the load would without doubt be over the handlebars in about one second. In addition, you were probably doing fifteen miles an hour. The situation was looking a bit grim at this stage.

The trick was to wait until something "gave." Worse still, if you happened to have a fixed pedal bike, where the pedals just kept going around regardless, you were really in very deep shit indeed.

The bottom of your coat was now well entrenched in the sprocket and chain. The coat's belt, which had a steel buckle and entrapment spike, was closing inwards and downwards on your hips. The rain hood was pulling down from the nape of your neck. The front of the hood, down on your forehead to just above your eyes, was now tilting your head back and your bum and spine were being pulled down into the bike seat.

It seemed that you almost knew what it was like to be a bit of corned beef, all strung up, ready to go into the pot, except "you" were still alive. The worst was yet to come.

The tension was leading to sheer panic. Your mind in overtime, what should you do now? Fall off on purpose, can't, you will break the glass in the thermos flask. Chance it and wait for something to give? Can't, the hood will either rip your head off or the raincoat belt will cut you in half. You can barely breathe. Pray for the chain to break perhaps.

Then like an un-leashed coil spring, the oilskin splits from the back bottom hem to the collar. Your face is still pointing skyward. All that is keeping up the forward momentum and upright balance is the speed of the bike, which is being guided along by the indented sheep track.

By this time the net handle, which had been resting over your shoulder, has tilted backwards, extending your right arm to its fullest. The bottom of your net is now sitting on the top of the rear mudguard. The sleeve of the oilskin on your right arm is up past the elbow. Still the sprocket chomps its way through the oilskin, which is now winding around the smaller rear sprocket.

There is only one thing worse than getting the bottom of your raincoat caught in the chain of your pushbike as you peddle along the gouged out sheep tracks. I will discuss that further on in the story!

You decide to let go of the net's handle but in doing so the end of the handle zooms up the open sleeve of the coat. The net slips off the back of

the mudguard, swings sideways, and hits the ground. It then bumps up off the ground and catches an overhead willow branch. The net handle carries on its merry way, up the sleeve, through the armhole and across your chest. Things are getting reasonably serious at this point.

The bike keeps going. Your chest does not, but your feet do and disengage themselves from the pedals. Your shins hit the undersides of the handlebars. The bike then does a back flip and you land on your back in the mud. The coat is still caught in the sprocket. The bike lands on top of you with the pointy end of the seat squarely in your crotch.

You lie there in the mud, crotch numb, winded, lungs screaming for breath, wondering how many ribs the handle of the net has broken. You optimistically think you've almost made it but then you hear the sickening tinkle of the glass shattering in the thermos. Then your shins start to throb like hell where they hit the handlebars.

What could possibly be worse? (All in good time!)

The weather clears and early the next morning you set off again. This time, no raincoat, a borrowed bike and a new thermos. No moon but the dynamo light on the borrowed bike sheds a good light. The new torch is much more powerful than the one you had broken the day before. The lights lead the way down through the sheep tracks and under the overhanging willow trees, between the gorse bushes. So far so good.

Yesterday's rain has left puddles in some of the minor depressions in the sheep track. With the aid of the tracks, the bike trundles along as if on a rail. You splash through the puddles with glee awaiting each new one to try to make a bigger splash. With yesterday's problems hardly a memory, you spy another puddle and push the pedals harder.

The front wheel hits the puddle and all of a sudden, bang! You are flying through the air, net, billy, backpack and, oh no, the new thermos. You land heavily in a gorse bush and look back. The bike is cart-wheeling straight at you from behind! You somehow dodge the flying bike, and ponder ...

... What the hell was that? Whatever it was, it was "the one thing worse than getting your raincoat caught in the chain of the bike!"

You extricate yourself from the prickles of the gorse bush and limp back in the direction you came from. You try to find the cause of the crash. It is still pitch dark and after locating your torch with a cracked lens, you cannot find any sort of obstruction. You are looking for things such as a wire across the track or a similar type of obstacle placed along it by a person, or persons unknown.

You pick up your gear and your bike. The bike's front wheel has a slight buckle but it still works in spite of the fact that on every revolution, the tyre scrapes on the forks. You ride on looking for the next puddle, this time ensuring that you skirt around it. You have now figured that someone had dug a hole in the last puddle, the probable reason for the crash.

Ahead you spy another puddle. You are again riding at quite a pace as you have lost time. It's starting to get light and you don't want to miss securing a good fishing position.

As you near the puddle, you hoist on the handlebars, ride out of the track and skirt the puddle. All of a sudden, bang, again! The same "someone" had deduced that by now you would have figured out, that there had been a hole dug in the last puddle. He knew that you would skirt this one. So he had dug another hole in the detour beside the puddle and covered it with twigs and grass.

Sean Horgan must have been here before you.

Over the handlebars you go, this time landing in another gorse bush but not before sliding through a mound of cowshit with no oilskin raincoat to protect you. The net is caved in, your pride is shattered and still you have not got anywhere near the river. Moreover, you stink! Once again, you sit and ponder your predicament. Then you hear the familiar tinkle of the glass in the thermos flask shattering as if in delayed shock. You locate its glass-filled shell in your backpack and hurl it into the bushes. You silently

remind yourself that next time, if there ever is a next time, to buy one of the newly invented stainless steel models without a glass inner.

The bike's front wheel is now square and you decide that whitebaiting is just not worth the bloody hassle. At this stage, eyes blurred from tears now rolling down your cheeks, you scout around looking for your gear. You are now tempted to throw the squashed net and buggered bike into the river.

You walk the lonely track, dragging the mangled bike and net back to the main road. Then trudge the two miles back into town. The sun is now up and you pull your beanie down over your eyes to avoid recognition from passers by.

From now on, you have decided to pay ten bob a pound and buy your whitebait from the Horgan boys. Let's face it, the hole in the puddle trick sure cures old age puddle runners!

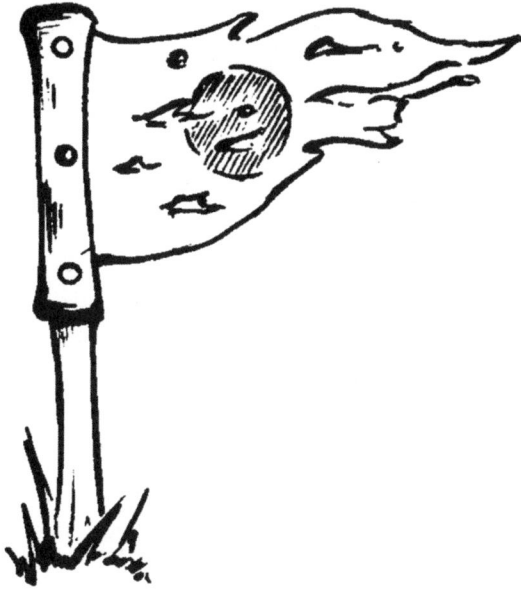

Bondy

Bondy lived two houses past us, on the same side of the street. His parents' house also had an exit to the park or cricket ground out through the back garden gate.

Bondy was an expert with an air rifle and owned one, which was almost as powerful as a .222 calibre rifle he reckoned. In hindsight that sure was a bit of an overstatement. I always wondered why it was called a "Volt 60" but learned later that it was a "Faulk 60". Probably a leftover from the war, I thought at the time. He also had a slug pistol, which seemed to be the size of a .44 Magnum. It was rumoured that he ended up shooting people for a living on behalf of the New Zealand Government in Malaya, but not with slug guns. A job right up his alley I thought.

Around the perimeter of the cricket ground, marking the boundary, were little wooden pegs. Each one had a triangular linen flag, half the size of

a handkerchief, tacked to it. There were three tacks to each flag. Bondy would take three shots at each peg with either of his guns and the flag would fall to the ground. He could do this from fifty yards away.

The cricket club must have often wondered why, and how, the flags became separated from the pegs. After many replacements they made the flags with a pouch which fitted over the peg. The flags were then tacked to the pegs as well. Bondy once told me that he was a bit pissed off about that.

Therefore, to counter this and to further his target practice he painted red dots on each of the flags and took pot shots at them instead. He said it reminded him of the red dots on the wings of Japanese warplanes he had heard about during the war. That was when he was just a youngster and he had also seen the planes in war comics with the same insignia.

The cricket club must have been pissed about their shredded flags from then on, but at least they lasted a bit longer than their predecessors.

Bondy's Belching Club

Bondy's Belching Club or the "BBC" had an elite membership of six. Although the membership was small, it was all quality. I did not have enough grunt to my belches to become a member. Only my brother Sean and my youngest sister Francie qualified to join from our family. Even Bondy's younger brother, Graham, could not gain membership. They did a lot of training, generally in the evenings.

Bondy was a huge bloke, not fat, just big. I don't remember what he did, or where he worked. He was at least ten years older than I was. Like ours, his house had a front verandah with a corrugated iron unlined roof. They were perfect venues for belching. The acoustics were excellent.

The belching contests had a curtain raiser. This consisted of my sister Francie and Graham Bond opening up all the doors and windows at the front of our houses. Then, as both played piano exceptionally well, they would play "duelling pianos". The result was the equivalent of *"Duelling Banjos"* in the movie, *Deliverance*. This went on for about ten minutes while the BBC members were warming up their belching techniques under their respective front verandas. Lummy, down at Grandma Hewitt's place, Bondy at his place and Sean at ours.

Francie would be punctuating her piano with the odd grunting belch. Dennis and Roger Crisp next door, the fifth and sixth members of the BBC were ready for their famous "Belchers Duet." This was set to the tune of *"Seventy Six Trombones."*

It was a sight to hear, "so to speak," and for fifteen minutes non-stop there were some of the best belches ever belched.

My favourite song in belch was belched to the tune of the *Blue Danube*. The pianists would crank out the first five notes and then the belchers would come in with, "Belch, belch – Belch, belch."

Francie and Graham were both talented young musicians who had their letters in piano. This meant that they were so good that they were supposedly able to teach piano and be paid for it.

Non-members of the BBC in the neighbourhood seemed to put up with the belching simply because they liked the music of the duelling pianos. The neighbours who didn't like it never complained. They knew that if they did, their roofs would field the odd rock or two for a few nights thereafter!

Mum who hated the whole thing, labelled the BBC as a bunch of "Piggish Larrikins." She called it a "filthy piggish trick." However, she was like that and had no sense of humour, for anything slightly on the "off side."

Members of the BBC reckoned that their form of belching was an art, sort of poetry in motion. Others did not.

Sometimes Bondy would be out in the back garden and let rip with a huge belch. Sean or Francie would hear it and return the call. This would go on for some time – communicating in belch across the neighbourhood.

Bondy once said that belching was an absolutely fascinating and riveting method of communication and totally code unbreakable. Obviously, you had to be a member of the BBC elite to be able to understand the language of belch. Sort of "belch ESP," I guess. Bondy never explained that though, and no one, ever questioned Bondy!

Slug Guns, Shanghais and Cattys

We moved on from catapults or "cattys" to shanghais and then to slug guns in a very short space of time. For various reasons, however, we seemed to always come back to cattys. Our first slug gun was an old Dianna 15. It was so gutless that you could almost catch the bullet in your teeth by firing the gun and then running after the bullet or slug!

Catapults were our favourite weapon, simply because they cost nothing to make, nothing for ammunition and were easy to hide. A leather tongue, cut from an old shoe, a length of rubber from a bike or car tube and a couple of bits of green fishing line were all that were required to make one. I remember once getting into all sorts of strife for cutting the tongue out of one of Dad's good dress shoes for the pouch of the catty!

To the average kid, cattys were highly inaccurate and could backfire on you. We spent hours using them and got to the stage where we could knock a bird out of a tree, or now and again, nail one in full flight. Hitting a stray cat on the prowl was relatively easy as we were experts.

Mum hated both cats and cattys but she couldn't have her cake and eat it too we thought, if she didn't want cats in her garden. The main reason she hated cattys was because the ammunition or "ammo" was stones. A pocket full of stones in her washing was not good news for the owner of the pants.

We didn't have a washing machine until the early sixties. Mum used to do all the washing by hand and then put it through the wringer. A device, which did exactly that, wring all the excess water out of the washed garment. Stones in pants pockets did not go down well in either process!

We would line up bottles on fences and shoot them down with ease. There was nothing worse, however, than when one of the strings holding the pouch on to the rubber broke. This was called a backfire and shit did the rubber sting when it came back at you, or when the stone in the pouch spun back and caught you in the face.

Sean was pretty good with a catty and could shoot from the hip with accuracy. I recall Sean, Kerry, me and our mate Lummy from down the street, taking out all the windows in an abandoned house. Well we thought it was abandoned, until the local cop came to visit the old man with his "suspicions".

There were a few nosey parkers in the town, forever trying to dob us to the cops. We were shown the local jail on many occasions and to an eight year old, it seemed like the end of the earth. The cop would drag us down there and we slowed down a pace or two after each visit. Hindsight, however, tells me that we could have busted our way out of it in a few minutes. It was just a small dunny type shed, the walls of which were tongue and grooved timber. The jail was only meant for drunks to sober up in.

Some of the other kids had shanghais but these were hard to hide, especially at school. The best end result with a shanghai was when we replaced the standard ammo with fencing staples. (Normally we used stones or marbles the latter of which we had an endless supply.) The staple went end over end in the air and could make a hell of a mess of washing on a clothesline, or to a heavily laden fruit tree.

As previously mentioned our mate Bondy, of the BBC fame, had a hell of a powerful slug gun. It fired bigger lead waisted pellets than normal. Bondy reckoned it could easily kill a cat at a hundred yards.

Slugs were not cheap to buy for our old Dianna 15 and so we cut up short lengths of number 8 wire as substitutes. This was probably the cause of the almost uselessness of the gun. The wire pellets had demolished what rifling there was in the barrel and so the passage through the barrel was a smooth one. The slug did not spin and the wire substitutes were sloppy in the barrel letting too much air escape or something.

One afternoon some really bad kids from another part of town came into the cricket ground with slug guns. One had a high-powered slug pistol as well. We were in for it this time and they had us bailed up behind a big Oregon fir tree. They were shooting at us from fifty yards away. They were for real. I never did find out what Sean had done to get these blokes so upset! They had deliberately come out of their territory, which was rare, especially in daylight. We used to venture into their territory, but only at night. They had obviously come here to sort us out once and for all. They were two or three years older than us and had a lot more fire power.

One of our mob, Richard Peychers, stuck his head out from behind a tree to see if it was safe to make a run for it and caught a slug dead centre between the eyes. I can still picture it. Here was Richard staring blankly at us with a slug buried up to the hilt in his forehead and a trickle of blood starting to run down past his nose. He went deadly white and both he and his brother fainted on the spot. With slugs zinging around us like bees, Sean calmly bent down and plucked the slug from Richard's forehead, wiped the blood off it on his jeans and pocketed it. "Might fit the Dianna," he said.
With all the commotion going on, Bondy heard it from his house and

came to save us with his Faulk 60. He poked the gun through the latch hole in his back gate and fired twenty or so rounds in rapid succession at the kids who had us bailed up. From their yells and screams, he must have got a couple of them. Bondy would probably not have cared if he had killed them. He would be immune from the law because he was so big. He probably would have buried the bodies in the back garden as well. He was fearless, just like Mr Wilkes, the local bank manager and keen gardener, who lived a few houses in the other direction from Bondy. Mr Wilkes was reputed to have shot and buried thirteen cats under his vegetable patch. A real Wyatt Earp!

Trout

One of Dad's great loves was trout fishing. He knew every inch of the riverbanks of the Motueka River and many other rivers and lakes in the northern part of New Zealand's South Island.

During the trout season he would be out fishing the Motueka River early in the morning before work. He'd come home for breakfast, go to work and then return to the river again in the evenings. The season started on the first day of October and lasted until the end of March. He brought home at least 500 trout every season ranging from two and a half to ten pounds in weight. The small ones he threw back into the river.

Most anglers had their favourite lures. His was the "Golden Devon". On at least two occasions, I recall him catching a sizeable trout and in its mouth was another lure. Both times the lure was an old one of his. He had a marking system for all of his lures and made many of them himself.

He had obviously hooked the fish some time prior, the trace had broken, and the fish given an extended life.

We got sick of eating bloody trout. It seemed that Mum knew a hundred ways to cook them, from deep and pan frying to sousing, and she sometimes disguised them with other foods.

Dad had names for most of his fishing spots. Many of these he made up himself and most were based on the owners of the farms through which the rivers ran. "Out the back of Frys", "Boy's Home", "Maggie Humphries", "Hewitt's", "Alexander Bridge", " Kohatu Pub", (not much fishing done at that spot), "McLean's", and so on.

Every time Dad went fishing, he would always tell Mum where he was going to be. He would say that he was off to have a "poke" in a given fishing spot. This meant that he would visit a fishing spot to test it out and either stay there, if he thought the conditions were right, or move on to another spot. I'd often go with him. So would the local parish priest, whom Dad introduced to trout fishing and who became a trout fishing fanatic.

I will never forget the evening Dad came home from work, changed into his fishing gear and as he walked out of the back door, he said to Mum, "I'm off to have a poke in Maggie Humphries' hole!" Kerry, Veronica, Francie and I almost dropped dead! Dad never intended the meaning we got and Mum would never have connected.

The Humphries had a farm some ten miles up the river. It was one of Dad's favourite fishing spots and was located at a bend with a huge whirlpool and a deep hole. He caught many large trout there.

The Yank Tank

In 1958 Dad had somehow acquired a 1929 Chrysler. I think he paid seventy quid for it. It was a big old American car, one like Elliot Ness and the *"Untouchables"* used to race around in. The only difference was that Dad's did not have any bullet holes in it.

The only changes to its original condition were huge steel-rimmed wheels and wide tyres, which had replaced the wooden spoked rims and skinny tyres. The seats were leather. When you sat in the back seat and stretched your feet out you couldn't reach the back of the front seat with your toes. It was Dad's pride and joy and he called it the "Yank Tank".

He just loved to drive the old Chrysler. It was unique and everyone knew Dad and would wave to him as he drove along and he'd wave back. He always drove the car at thirty miles an hour. Everywhere! It had a speedometer, which was like a compass. The miles per hour would show as numbers on a revolving glass ball, which you could see through a little oblong hole in the dashboard. It also had a lever on the steering wheel, which read, "Spark Advance" and "Spark Retard." He reckoned he didn't know what that was for and never used it. None of us kids had a clue what it was for either.

Countless times we tried to egg him on to make the car go faster. Like thirty-one or even thirty-two miles an hour but he would just grin and keep driving at thirty! His right foot was the equivalent of the modern day cruise control.

Dad came home from the Post Office for lunch most days. Some days he drove the Chrysler to work, back for lunch and then back to work. The drive time each way was only about two minutes and he could get to the Post Office just as quickly by walking through the park via the gate out the back of our place.

When he came home for lunch, Dad would drive the car up the driveway and park in front of the garage. It would always be exactly two minutes past noon. He would then go inside for lunch.

Mum would meet him at the car and as soon as he stepped out she'd be talking away about everything and anything. He would be nodding his head every now and again and rarely said a word in reply. This was for two reasons. The first was that he couldn't get a word in edgeways even if he tried. The second was that this was a ritual, a habit that had gone on for thirty-five years. I am sure that Dad never heard a single thing she said but had the ability to let her think he did! Somewhere, however, in the back of his mind or subconscious the important bits must have registered. Simply because when Dad did ask her something, I never ever heard her say, "I told you about that last week!"

After lunch he normally walked out into the vegetable garden to "check out the spuds" or spend a few minutes watering the garden. While wandering around having a smoke, there'd be Mum, right on his heel, yakking away again.

At three minutes to one he'd walk to his car, get in and fire it up via a kick-start on the floor next to the accelerator. He'd half turn so that he could see his way while reversing out the driveway. Mum would be still talking while walking beside the car as he reversed out of the drive. She stopped talking only when the car went faster than she could walk. She never seemed offended that he had gone off when she had not finished, but she was never finished talking so I guess Dad thought that was OK.

They both knew that the one-way conversation would continue where she left off when he came home after work via the pub, or when he got home for lunch the next day.

Except when Mum was in one of her famous "mute modes," she could really talk. In fact, she practically talked all of the time and for someone with this habit, she did not talk rubbish. This was unusual for most people who talk most of the time. If you had the time to listen, you could learn all sorts of amazing things, as she was very intelligent. She had a great command of the English language and was a walking encyclopaedia. When it came to plants and trees, she could name almost all of them. Not only by their English or common name but also by their botanical name.

The routine was always the same until one day in about 1966 as he was leaving, Mum must have been standing too close to the side of the car. It had big running boards which you stepped on to get into it. Mum's feet were under these and as Dad reversed out the driveway, he ran over her feet!

He was half turned, looking out towards the road and the noise of the old straight eight engine drowned out her shrieks and screams of agony. Two tons of "Yank Tank" over both feet was a bit much and she collapsed in a heap in the driveway.

Dad got to the street and looked left and right, backed across the street and drove off to work. He had done this a million times before and so had Mum but not the last bit! She was lying in the driveway with both feet crushed and broken. The kids weren't home and the neighbours on both sides were at work.

It took her an hour to drag herself inside the house and another hour to claw her way, via the phone stool, up the wall to the phone. During this time she lapsed in and out of consciousness wondering what the hell had happened and most of all why Dad didn't see her and stop.

She had to ring the telephone exchange, get through to Dad, and have him call the doctor. He thought that while the doctor fixed her up he had a good excuse to bugger off to the pub. After all, what could he do about it? Shoot the car perhaps.

It took Mum months to recover and she always walked "a bit funny" after that.

I was away at college at the time but I remember my younger sisters saying that Dad's standard of cooking was bloody awful during her recuperation period and they were landed with a hell of a lot of extra work while Mum couldn't walk.

In spite of it all, Mum never lost her voice!

The Motorbike

As a young boy, I never really liked motor bikes. My brother Sean changed that because he had one and so, when the time came, I had to have one. He was my hero and I knew that one day I would certainly get one. Mine had to be exactly the same as his. I could never afford one, as I couldn't save my money, but being the youngest son, there just might be a way round that.

Dad had a motorbike when he was about our age and so did my oldest brother Pat. He broke his leg on his motorbike and almost killed his pillion passenger as well, so Mum told us. By this time, he was away in the army so I never heard the full story.

Mum hated the "bloody things", she said, and this was one of the few times she swore. She always referred to them as "bloody motorbikes".

My brother Kerry was away at college or in the seminary trying to become a priest at the time. He could have been an All Black like Grandad or represented New Zealand in rugby league like Dad had. But he wasn't and he didn't because he was Kerry and he had many other dreams to fulfil. It seemed he had a more important role to play in this world than just to save a few souls, or play serious football. Both would have been splendid of course. You see, he was the one who egged us on and played a major part in many of the hi-jinks. Especially the ones during our late teens and early twenties.

Anyway, back to the motorbike! It was my fifteenth birthday. I had borrowed a little green BSA Bantam 100cc motorbike from a friend. I rode it down to the licensing office of the local Transport Department.

I had been riding motorbikes and driving cars for years prior to this and had it all worked out on how to pass my driving test on my fifteenth birthday. You can get a driving licence as soon as you are fifteen years old in New Zealand. In those days it was pretty easy to get one. There was no probationary period and L-plates were not required.

My brother Sean said that, "All you have to do is stand six feet away from a wall chart with a piece of cardboard over one eye and read out loud a few jumbled letters that become smaller in size. You then have to repeat the process with the cardboard over the other eye. Don't be a smart arse when you are doing the eye test like I had been, and read out the name in tiny print at the bottom of the chart which says, *Printed by WE Owen, Govt., Printing Office Wellington*," he said!

"The cop will ask you five questions about the road rules. You have to get three correct. The cop will then get in the car with you and drive around the streets for five minutes or so. If you are going for a motorbike licence, he is supposed to follow you in his car around a couple of the town's streets. Then you get your licence as long as you pay him five shillings."

Dad was the "Acting" Postmaster at the time whatever that meant, and he must have felt quite good about it. Being the "Acting" boss meant that he could go out for a stroll down the street from time to time. He had to walk about one hundred yards to the Transport Department office. This would take him about half an hour because he would stop and chat to most of the people he met along the way. He agreed to meet me at the office of the Transport Department.

When I arrived, the local cop was talking to Dad. He didn't seem to notice that I had ridden there on the motorbike without a licence. Maybe he didn't care, or his conversation with Dad was a lot more important than my test or my riding a motorbike without a licence.

The cop told me to ride my bike around the block. When I returned he told me to go round again. He had seen me riding motorbikes and cars around the streets for years and knew as well as I did that this was just a waste of his time.

Obviously, the conversations about the local postal situation and traffic conditions were of vital importance. They took precedence over an enthusiastic fifteen year old's desire for his motor cycle licence. Maybe they were talking about more important issues such as football or trout fishing. Whatever the topic was, it did the trick. When I got back from my second trip around the block, the cop with the beer gut and black hat told me to hop upstairs and see the clerk. She happened to be one of my older sister's girlfriends.

She had huge breasts. That was all I knew about birds' things under blouses at the time. I knew about that because I remember Mum's when I got the odd glimpse some years before when it was feeding time for my younger sisters. Mum's were fairly big but just average to the ones I was now confronted with. I kind of had a funny feeling about this bird but didn't fully understand why. I would find out soon enough when motorbikes and sport played second fiddle to birds.

She didn't give me the eye test that Sean had warned me about. At least I don't think she did. Probably because she could tell straight away that there was nothing the matter at all with my eyes!

I had been practising for weeks with a scrawl I called my signature. "The Breasts" told me to sign three times and that was it. I now had my motorbike, car and truck licences. She ticked three of the five boxes on the licence because she was a "friend of my sisters" she said. She even asked me if I wanted a bus or bulldozer licence. "The Breasts" then demanded five bob and I told her that Dad would be up in a minute to fix that bit up.

The fat traffic cop and the Acting Post Master were still deep in conversation when I grinned my way down the stairs and out on to the pavement. I told Dad that "The Breasts" needed five shillings and I was off!

Two weeks later there it was. The most beautiful sight I had seen in fifteen years. A 500cc Triumph Speed Twin. The details of how it got to be standing on its double stand in our back yard are a secret to this day. In fact, they are as much a secret as its disappearance some six weeks later. In both cases no one will ever know, because those who did, have now passed away.

The bike and I went to school together the next day. We went home together. We held hands constantly for a few weeks and then we parted as quickly as we had come together. A scenario I would get used to, but not with motorbikes, over the next few years!

After a couple of weeks of getting to know each other, the bike developed a kind of a squeaky farting noise. One of the mufflers seemed to be faulty. This was probably because of my little party trick. I had discovered that if you stuffed diesel soaked dunny paper up the exhaust pipes with a broom handle and then took off at speed, you would leave a smoke screen of more intensity than the local sawmill's waste burner. It was a very effective way to make your exit from the school bike park. Sometimes expressly performed for the country kids waiting for the bus to take them home. Bloody show-off!

Another kid at school had a Triumph much like mine but it was a couple of years older. He told me that he had a spare muffler and that I could have it. Andrew Macleod lived about four miles out of town on a farm. He said that he would help me fit the muffler after school one afternoon in his Dad's workshop.

On the way out to the farm, I decided to see how fast the bike would go. I rode through the town speed limits and out into the open road. A round disc on a wooden post some ten feet off the ground indicated this. As you left the township, the disc was painted black and white, which meant you could now travel at speeds up to fifty-five miles an hour. When entering the township from the other direction, the disc was red and white which meant that the speed limit was thirty miles an hour. Some of the red signs had the numerals "30" painted in the centre, others didn't. Tough on a colour-blind person if the numerals were not there I always thought.

I was almost flying at eighty-five miles an hour dressed in my school uniform of shoes, socks, shorts, shirt and jumper. For some sort of hand protection, I added a pair of elbow length leather gloves and a crash helmet. This was designed along the lines of a World War II German soldier's helmet. Helmets were not compulsory in those days and Sean had left me the cool legacy of letting the helmet straps hang loose and undone. The only problem with this was that at speed the straps and buckle would flick away at your cheeks and sting like hell. But I was tough!

Apart from the strange noises from the muffler, the bike ran well. A new muffler may even make it go faster. I remember flashing past the green fields dotted with sheep. In one paddock in particular there were four sheep close to the fence. It was as if an image of the scene was posted in my memory for instant recall sometime in the near future.

We fitted the new muffler and I thanked my friend and started for home. It was about 6.30 p.m. and the sun was setting behind me over a hill known as Brown Acre. In winter the summit, which was bare of vegetation, was often covered with snow. Its elevation, a mere three thousand feet. A baby, however, to some of the mountains further down south on the Island.

I felt free. Free of school and dorky teachers. It was a beautiful evening. The bike did go faster. I think perhaps a hundred miles an hour. The road markers flashed by. White posts blurred with the green background of food destined for wool. This in turn would be exported as carpet to the world and then the sheep, without the wool, as food for Poms. I learnt this at school.

I was dreaming and suddenly the window in my memory opened just in time for me to look up and to my right. The four sheep, previously inside the fence, had somehow managed to escape. They were now on the grass verge of the highway. Shit! They wouldn't, I thought. Would they? They did!

Another school friend, John Woodley who was destined to become a world champion 500cc motor cycle rider, would never have done what I did next. There was no time to think. Not even time to panic. No experience to call upon for this new rider. These four bloody sheep decided to cross the road from my right barely fifty feet in front of me. I was still doing ninety miles an hour.

They came across. The first two jogged head to tail, a gap of about three feet and then the second two, head to tail again. I aimed for the three-foot gap in the middle. I hit the brakes, both front and rear. I would have made it had the bike not gone sideways.

There was an enormous thump. I remember as I parted with the bike, an upside down view of the red glow of the sun setting above Brown Acre and that was all.

It was a strange sight as I stood on the road twenty yards from the speed sign. I was on the town side of the sign and yet the red circle on white background was facing me with a big "30" in the centre. This was all wrong.

It turned out that my body had hit the sign while I was flying through the air and had spun it one hundred and eighty degrees. Quite a feat I thought as I must have been ten feet in the air to achieve it. If I had hit the post that held the disc I would not be writing this!

What I could not figure out was that the actual impact site of the bike, the sheep and me, was more than 100 yards away on the "open road" side of the speed sign. Open road was another term meaning that you could travel at 55 miles per hour. How high must I have gone when I came off the bike? At least twenty feet perhaps! That's when I learned that, in future, I should not jump up in the air without an engine and propellor or at least a parachute.

I started to laugh for in the distance towards the hills, motionless on the roadway, were four sheep. Like a strike in a bowling alley, I had taken out the first two with the front wheel and the second two with the back wheel. Quite a feat once more I guess, and I was still alive!

Beyond the sheep, the farmer who owned them was running towards me and I kept laughing. I was still alive and I didn't feel a thing.

The bike was grinding and groaning on the grass verge and spinning like a top, wobbly and intoxicated at the end of its momentum. It had travelled the same distance as I had. Wow! This was incredible. How could I explain this one away to the oldies? Just as well the footy season was over. Something inside me had to be broken. My gloves were missing and so was my helmet.

The farmer arrived at the scene at the same time as another motorcyclist. No one said a word. We stood and stared at each other for what seemed like ages and the motorbike kept grinding and groaning in the grass. The farmer found my helmet and what was left of my gloves. These were reduced to shreds.

The helmet had a hole in it through which you could put your fist. The farmer said the sheep were all dead. He said that it was his fault because they should not have been on the road after sunset by law. That was interesting because the sun was neither up or down at the time but sort of half way. He knew the "Old Man", meaning Dad, and he said that he would pay to have the bike fixed. I still didn't say a word.

The farmer didn't say anything else. He climbed the fence and walked away to the farmhouse to get this tractor and trailer to collect the sheep. These would probably be for sale as prime fresh lamb at the "pig butchery" tomorrow. This particular butchery had a bunch of pink neon pigs running around the roof at night time.

As he walked across to the farmhouse, he turned a couple of times and shook his head. I'm sure I heard him say when he was almost at the farmhouse, "I heard the thump." I said to myself, "So did I!"

The bike finally died.

I never knew the name of the other motorbike rider who had stopped. Neither he, nor the farmer, asked me if I was hurt. He picked my bike up and said that it might still work. He ripped the front mudguard off and unbolted the mangled crash bars. We sort of straightened the handlebars and discarded numerous other bits and pieces. This left us with a thing that resembled a ladies pushbike, with an engine and a petrol tank.

He fired it up and reckoned it would be rideable. I straddled what was left of the seat, discovered I only had low gear, and slowly rode "The Beast" home. I don't know why I didn't turn to wave good-bye or yell a thankyou to the bloke who had stopped to help me. I just rode slowly home. Maybe I was too aware that I had escaped death by just a fraction and was in some sort of shock.

I chugged down the driveway of our house. A few feet before the open garage doorway I half fell, half jumped off the Trumpet, a nickname some people called Triumphs. I had renamed her "The Beast" and it was going to be hard to kill her. "The Beast" trundled on past Dad's 1929 Chrysler and expired when she hit the back wall of the garage.

We were both quite sick.

Mum must have been down the back garden somewhere. I sure as hell was in no mood to go and find her and nor did I want to! Dad walked down the back steps of the house, took one look at me and said, "I had a motorbike when I was your age, an old Army Indian. I hit a power pole. That's why I have never ridden on any of my sons' motorbikes." He then told me to go to bed, "before your mother sees you."

Some time later that night, I heard the phone ring and figured it must have been the farmer. Dad must have answered it.

I awoke twelve hours later. Christ! It was 8.30 a.m. I was stiff and sore and almost fell out bed. I had to get to school. I was still dressed! I blinked away the sleep and went to the kitchen. Mum looked at me kind of funny. I'm sure Dad wouldn't have betrayed me. She looked at what was left of my knees, caked with dry blood. She then asked why my toes were sticking out the end of my shoes. I hadn't even noticed those things or what was left of them. I offered some piss weak excuse or outright lie. Mum looked away and then turned to hand me my cut lunch. I tried to reach out to take the package but the pain in my right arm, chest and shoulder was unbearable.

Mum instantly accused me of coming off that "bloody motorbike." Too hard to hide this one, and by now I could taste the salt in my tears and vomit was on its way.

The hospital was thirty miles away. I had four broken ribs, a broken shoulder, miscellaneous cuts, bruises and serious grazes to my knees, hips and toes, and a pride almost beyond repair. After a short stay in hospital, they let me go home, but not before I had fallen in love with most of the young nurses. The feeling was probably not mutual.

A nursing sister even knitted me a sweater. I remember it well. It was royal blue with a black stripe around the middle of the chest and another one on each sleeve just above the elbow. She arrived at our place a couple of weeks later with the finished article and demanded four quid for it! Good on you Dad.

I stumbled around home for a week or so having my own private pity party. It was hard with a mother who had all of a sudden become stone deaf and had gone into one of her famous mute modes. She did this when she was pissed off about something. I bet even she couldn't have made the gap between the sheep, I thought.

The cuts and grazes on my kneecaps became infected and I had to go back to hospital for a couple of days. "Sister Knit" was on holiday and Dad breathed a sigh of relief.

This time when I arrived home, my ex best friend, "The Beast" was there. All bright and shiny, perched on its double stand on a pad under the carport. It looked as good as it did when I first laid eyes on it some weeks before. However, this time it seemed to be leering at me as if to say, "You can't destroy me that easily." Obviously not!

I could walk fairly well by this time but still had the rib and shoulder problem. The school break up dance was in a few days and I didn't want to miss it. I wouldn't have to dance though and that was good. I could just sit and perve at all the birds. I could revel in all the sympathy and hero worship I would get from my mates for killing four sheep on a motorbike and surviving!

The biggest problem was not being able to ride "The Beast". The first hurdle would be Mum. The second would be getting "The Beast" started, as my right knee was still not up to using the kick start.

Dad had been sick and had been home for a few days. His favourite place to sit and read the paper was on a deck chair under the carport. Here he'd sit and recover from hangovers or play crib with anyone who knew the game.

He now had the company of "The Beast" and me. Mum was slowly emerging from mute mode and told me that Dad had been covering that "bloody motorbike" up every night with a blanket, waiting for me to come home. He seemed so proud of its resurrection. She said he'd sit and stare at it all day. I bet he was secretly dreaming of giving it a run round the block when Mum went shopping. I was to find out a short time later that this was only wishful thinking.

It was mid-afternoon the next day and Dad and I were sitting out under the carport playing crib. We were discussing the possibility of whether the bike would still run as well as it did "pre-sheep". We had also received a letter from my brother Kerry, away at college, who asked if we had gone back to get the sheep. No mention as to my health because to him that would never be an issue.

We couldn't handle it any longer. Off came the cover and I gingerly climbed on "The Beast". There was no way I could use my right leg to kick-start the bike. Straddling it and willing it to fire up under its own accord just wasn't going to work. Electric start systems were not on Triumphs in 1965. Not on this model anyway.

Dad either felt sorry for me and thought that Mum was out of sight and hearing range. Or perhaps he had weakened after forty years of nightmares of old Army Indian motorbikes and power poles.

That's when I learned what empathy was, although the term was rarely used in those days. He never said a word as I slipped off the seat. He climbed on board as if he had been doing it every day and turned the ignition key to "on." I could see a twinkle in his eye and a slight smile as he positioned himself for the ride of his life.

Imagine if you will a single garage with a carport at the side. The eight by four-inch timber beams that hold up the iron roof of the carport are attached to the garage at right angles and are cut into another beam, which runs parallel to the garage wall. This beam in turn is supported by half a dozen four by four inch posts, similar to modern day pergola posts. "The Beast" is positioned in the centre of the carport.

Even after a good meal, Dad was only a little bloke. It was going to take a lot of grunt to fire up "The Beast". However, he had the persistence and stamina of a winner. He was the sort of bloke who once he had embarked on a mission, never gave up until he succeeded.

With his left foot, he clicked the gear lever to neutral, reached down, and turned both carburettor taps to the "on" position. He twisted the handgrip throttle to squirt some "juice" into the engine. He pulled the clutch in with his left hand and with his right foot, wound the kick-start slowly down, and then slowly up.

He performed this same manoeuvre once more but only to the half way point of the kick start's downward arc. He then let the kick start come slowly back up to the apex of its arc on its internal spring. This spring normally disengaged when the engine fired. He did all this with such polish that I reckon he must have been practising when Mum was not around!

The lights changed to green. He stood to his full five foot six inches with all his weight on the kick-start under his right foot. The rubber twist-grip throttle in his right hand was wound wide open. Something had to give here I thought.

It did. All hell broke loose! The clutch was out, the kick-start hit rock bottom but didn't stay there, as it should have done. It was on its way back up and Dad was on it! Twin piston engines rarely kick back but this time this one did.

In that split second, I saw the shock and horror of the unexpected in his eyes and the flash of white move like lightning across his face. At that moment, my empathy turned to sympathy and there was nothing I could do. He was on his way to the ceiling or heaven, which ever came first. The eight by four, timber roof beam did! Dad never got to pass go or collect the two hundred dollars.

About the time the beam was being embedded in his head, another interesting thing happened. There was a hell of a backfire through the carburettors and two monstrous sheets of flame spurted twenty feet out behind "The Beast". It was lucky that Dad was in the air at the time or his legs would have been burnt as well. One of the carburettors melted and the seat and saddlebags caught fire.

Dad had now fallen to the ground like a sack of spuds and was away with the fairies. I couldn't do much to help and started to laugh.

Mum had been hand watering the vegetable garden with the hose while we were planning our attack on "The Beast". She had now made her way to within watering range.

The explosion gave her a hell of a fright, made her turn and upon seeing the fire, she tried to hose it down. Dad was not moving. The fire got bigger and was now on the creeper on the carport. Mum's prized clematis. That's all Dad and I needed!

"The Beast's" wiring was the next to go and that was like fifty or so of the hand held sparklers we set off during Guy Fawkes Night.

Mum's hose was now on the clematis. Flowers were far more important than "bloody motorbikes", husbands or kids it seemed. She was yelling, screaming and jumping up and down.

Dad was now half on his feet staggering around the lawn letting out little grunts and wondering what the hell hit him. I had managed to throw a canvas ground sheet over "The Beast". None of us really knew what to do next. Especially Dad! He was right out of it sitting on the concrete pathway, leaning up against the house, now looking like a sack of mashed spuds. Boy, I thought, he was sure going to get it when Mum stopped hosing and screaming.

It all settled down after a while. "The Beast" smouldered away for an hour or so and I knew then that its days were well and truly numbered.

Eventually Dad got to his feet by clawing his way up the weatherboards on the side of the house. He wandered around the lawn in circles, mumbling incoherently for a while. Finally he made his way down through the back garden and went out through the gate and into the park. He snuck off to the pub and wasn't home before I went to bed. Mum was really pissed about the whole thing. She returned to mute mode.

I didn't know whether to laugh or run. I burst out laughing. However, if I could have run away, I would have.

I managed to get myself to school the next morning and sat in Lloyd Goodall's maths class pondering possible reasons for the slight technical problem with "The Beast". All I could put it down to was the fact that its timing was all to hell after the re-construction and left it at that. When I came home from school that day "The Beast" was gone, never to be seen again.

To the day they died, "The Beast" was never ever mentioned by Mum, Dad and definitely not by me in their presence. As they say in *Readers Digest*, "A life's not worth that."

Birds

Mum was always on at my brother Sean and me about all the girlfriends we had. Not that she minded us having girlfriends but she did not like the fact that we had multiple girlfriends on the go, at the same time. I didn't have a problem with it! I saw it as a game which you really had to keep on top of, especially in a small town.

We did have a problem with Mum however, and although she would not admit it, I think she used to play her own little game trying to sabotage ours. It was like trying to play two games of chess at the same time. Now and again, she would stymie us and one day she really cleaned me out.

Every year Motueka High School held inter-school sports with others of similar size in the South Island. The main schools involved were Lincoln High, just out of Christchurch, and Buller High, which is on the West Coast.

These tournaments lasted three days, Thursday, Friday and Saturday. The grand finale on Saturday night was a dance party for all the participants, plus the non-playing senior students from the host school.

Heaps of "new talent" arrived and many hearts got broken. Being a member of the rugby first fifteen was a plus they said, especially if you won. No matter how ugly you were, your chances of success before, during or after the dance, or all three, were fairly reasonable. This was some sort of myth handed down from team to team. Certainly was a myth as far as I was concerned!

I had spent a year locked away at St Kevin's College. This is a Catholic boarding school for boys, three hundred odd miles from Motueka, in a town called Oamaru. While there, I was fortunate enough to play for the first fifteen rugby side, reputed to be at the time, the best in the country. At the end of that year, just prior to exams, I got appendicitis and missed sitting my school leaving exams. I had also applied to join the police force the following year. Some complications after the appendix operation forced me to miss the intake. So I had another year to sit around twiddling my thumbs until the next intake.

I had a choice of whether to pick tobacco, then fruit and go whitebait fishing or go back to school at Motueka High, play rugby, and go whitebaiting both before and during the season!

The rugby coach was Don Blyth, a local high school teacher and ex army officer. Don conned me into going back to school to sit for my exams, which I somehow passed. He wanted to get me into his school rugby first fifteen and probably couldn't care less about my schooling.

It turned out to be a great year for playing football, playing up, and whitebaiting.

I can't recall having a steady girlfriend. I do remember having three unsteady ones however, all at the same time as Lincoln High came to visit us for the annual inter-school sports events.

The bird from Lincoln High was quite a challenge. It seemed that some of my mates were contemplating the same thing as I was! Mum found out on day two of the sports event, via her normal gossip hotline, that I had cottoned on to a new bird. One of my sisters told her that I was "in love" again, with a girl from Lincoln. That particular sister, "she should talk!"

It was Saturday afternoon and we had won the rugby. Tonight was the dance. All I had to do was stay away from a couple of local birds and a third, who was away in Nelson, some thirty miles away at another school, and no one would ever know. The following Monday things would be back to normal, girl wise, I thought!

I got home from the football and bugger me! Who should be sitting with "Mother"' in front of the open fire in the lounge, sipping tea and having a grand old chat? Two of the prettiest girls in the district, the ones I thought were my girlfriends, plus the "challenge" from Lincoln High and the lass from Nelson College for Girls. "She just happened to be home for the weekend," Mum told me later.

With the help of one of my sneaky younger sisters, Mum had rounded them all up for a "checkmate". I bolted!

The dance that night was not one to remember. Word had spread and not even the ugly chicks would talk to me.

Nothing like starting afresh, I guess, but unattached good-looking birds were getting bloody hard to find around Mot after that. Just as well I was off to Wellington the following January to the Police Academy. "And Wellington was reputed to be a big city with heaps of girls," I consoled myself.

Gwip The Chithel

Fred Meagre had a slight lisp and was known affectionately as "Gwip the Chithel" by all of the students to whom he taught woodwork. What a great teacher he was. I was fortunate to be in his class. Two of my brothers, Pat and Sean had preceded me and both had performed well academically. I think Fred felt sorry for me!

It is my understanding that in the later years of Fred's teaching career, he mellowed a bit and stopped throwing lumps of four by two timber, and the odd chisel, at any kid who misbehaved.

In his technical drawing classes, Fred would walk the classroom between the aisles of connected drawing boards and look down at our drawings from an upside down perspective. He'd often point out that my base lines were too heavy. "They need to be invithible," he'd say, and spray about a gallon of spittle over the blueprint. I'd look up at him and before I could reply he'd beat me to it and say, "Don't be thilly Pat, Thean, Nick and don't arthk me ... 'If I make them invithible, how can I highlight them later?'" So I didn't ask!

Aside from being a member of the first fifteen rugby team at Mot High, the only real highlight or prize I ever won at school was the "Practical, Theory and Technical Drawing Award", presented upon graduation.

The class grading system at the high school was based on an A, B, G system. "A" was for future academics, teachers, doctors etc. "B" was for future trades people, farmers and business operators. "G" was for general workforce. I was in the B group.

I remember Fred taking me aside one day and he said that "B" was for "Betht" and don't you forget it thon. Motht of thothe in "A" will turn out ath profethionalth, layabouth, dole bludgerth, draft dodgerth and teacherth, and none of them will be able to change a light bulb or hammer in a nail! A few, like your brotherth Pat and Thean will do extheptionally well ath Army Colonelth and thuccthessful entrepreneurth". His last words were, "The "B'th" will be the productive oneth who build economieth and that the otherth will hang off that!"

At that point, I made the excuse that I was late for football practice and "lithped" my way through training! In hindsight, what Fred said that day, is almost exactly what happened. I didn't turn out to be a tradesman. I could have been a carpenter or a gardener if I wanted to and I can also change a light bulb! Fred did have a bit of inside info in his predictions however, because my brother Pat was already a captain in the army well before I left high school. Sean was always one who could work smart and extremely hard and save and spend his money wisely, from a very young age.

Memories Of Mot High and Saint Kevin's College

I don't have many of these but at Mot High my education revolved around rugby, woodwork and associated technical classes, English and geography. I was hopeless at maths but enjoyed the classes because of the teacher, Lloyd Goodall. He was also a Mot High Old Boy, having attended at the same time as my older brother Pat and sister Hilary.

I'd sit in his class with an absolute blank look on my face as Lloyd would expound his theories of algebra and trigonometry on the blackboard. At times he would turn to the class looking for some poor bugger to extend the math to the next stage. I'd want to duck down behind the desk or flip the lid up so he couldn't see and single me out. He knew damn well that I'd never in a million years have the answer.

He seemed to look at me first and then address the question elsewhere. I was grateful for that. His look however, always suggested that there was no way I was a sibling of Pat, Hilary or Sean, all of whom had sat in possibly the same seat as me, albeit some years before. They could probably have answered the questions in their sleep. My High School Certificate score in maths was 9% and while that seems pathetic, it turns out that it probably should have been about 70%. Lloyd confirmed this with me a couple of weeks after the exam. My failure was simply because I did not show my workings or in other words, how I got the result. To me maths was rather simple and most of the time I could look at the questions and work the answer out in my head. I'd then write it down. Not good enough for some yahoo in the Education Department who probably thought I was cheating. So I got zilch for the correct answer. If I remember correctly, the exam lasted two hours. I spent twenty minutes on the questions and left the exam room to head off whitebaiting as there was a good tide and it was nearing the end of the season!

My English teacher was Mr Mann. He was a great little bloke and also the Assistant Headmaster. I had a lot of time for him, performed well in his classes, and enjoyed reasonable results.

In geography, the teacher was Terry Miles. He also coached the second fifteen rugby side and was the perfect teacher. Again I enjoyed his classes and did reasonably well.

I have already covered my favourite subject, woodwork and technical drawing, with Fred Meagre.

It is interesting that my narrow pass in my final leaving certificate was based on the subjects I enjoyed. In hindsight, however, it was more the interpersonal skills and understanding of the teachers involved that got me through. I believe that the Education Department should take note of how important teacher student relationships are. The key must surely be the level of interpersonal skills as opposed to the level of the teacher IQ or their subject knowledge.

In 1966 my year at Saint Kevin's College revolved more around rugby and achieving the goal of making the first fifteen rugby team. At the time, Saint Kevin's had arguably the best college side in New Zealand. I did make the side, much to the disgust of some of the boys who had been there for all of their secondary education. There was some animosity towards me from my own schoolmates. Because of this a couple of injuries sustained in the matches I played for Saint Kevin's actually came from my own teammates! One was a broken and bloodied nose sustained in a ruck as payback from a player whose brother's spot I had taken. The second was a bite on the ear from the same player when I grabbed him by the gonads a couple of weeks later as payback for the nose job!

The reason for spending a year at Saint Kevin's was simply because I was not concentrating on my schooling in Mot as much as I should have. There were too many outside distractions. This combined with a school boy pre-dance piss up, to which some of the teachers over-reacted.

The highlight of my year at Saint Kevin's was the annual North vs South game. This was a traditional in-house fixture played at the end of the season between two teams selected from all the college players. Saint Kevin's is located in a town on the East Coast of the South Island called Oamaru in North Otago. An imaginary line was drawn from the college gates to a point on the West Coast of the South Island, near Hokitika.

The two teams were picked, one from south of the line and the other from north of the line. It was a bit lopsided in that 75% of the students came from south of the line and 70% of the first fifteen did as well. In the history of the college, of about a hundred years, the North had never beaten the South. Comparing the teams in ability was the equivalent of the All Blacks playing Italy. In this case, Italy being the North side.

The North had only five of the first fifteen players and the rest were in the South side. The five were Hoppy Inder from Queenstown, Andy Ryan and Peter O'Donnell from Timaru, Ian Dee from Nelson and me from Mot. For some reason, Queenstown was included in the North side's catchment area even though it is geographically south of the imaginary line. Obviously the Christian Brothers screwed up here but they were Australian and that probably explains it! Anyway we needed Hoppy. We needed all the help we could get and he was a damn good player

The South side had three players who would go on to become All Black trialists. The team included the Boyle clan from Otago, the McAtamneys from Central Otago, and the rest were farmers' sons from Southland. They were all big tough bastards.

The result of this particular game in 1966 was a 17 to 16 win to the North. I will never forget that game, in fact it was the best game of rugby I had ever been involved in. I kicked all but three of the points and Peter O'Donnell scored our only try. We were down by two points with a few seconds remaining on the clock. We were awarded a penalty on halfway, a little off centre of the goal posts, some 55 yards away. I kicked the goal and in the annual college magazine of that year, there is a photo of me doing so.

I tell this story about my year at Saint Kevin's simply to describe my determination to succeed in anything I attempted in the future. Nothing is impossible. There is no such thing as good luck I was told. Success is simply, the harder you work, the luckier you get. This has stood me in good stead in the years since Saint Kevin's.

During my time at Saint Kevin's I happened to read a "Wilber Smith" novel in which he wrote, "If you want to be a winner then you must avoid the company of losers, for their despair is contagious." This was in relation to animals in the wild and the survival of the fittest. I remember using the quote in front of my local parish priest during my late teens. Even though the quote is probably quite true, my audience of the priest was not quite the right setting for such a statement and it earned me a hefty clip around the ears!

Like everyone, I have made mistakes over the years but the positives outweigh the negatives. I have achieved very positive results in building successful sales teams in Auckland, New Zealand and across Australia during the past twenty-five years. Prior to that, my dogged hours spent on the practice greens of golf clubs around Canterbury, culminated in a reasonably high level of competence in that sport. Then I was fortunate enough to win my division of the world jet boat championships in Canada. These have all been highlights.

None would have been achieved had I not had the positive influences during my schoolboy years.

Remote Controls

As kids, we didn't have a television. The local priest had one and so did Grandma Hewitt down the street and we used to visit either one of their homes to watch it.

When I was in my last year of high school, I had a part time job working for a second hand furniture dealer.

A house lot of deceased estate furniture turned up one day and it included a near new black and white television. It was in a huge cabinet and had about ten knobs on the front. It was like an ancient radio, but bigger. The knobs adjusted everything from volume to "fuzziness" and horizontal and vertical hold. I managed to get the set in lieu of wages and gave it to Mum and Dad as their first television.

Years went by and we had all left home. One day I returned to visit my parents and was amazed to see Dad sitting in the lounge room, in his favourite armchair, watching that same old black and white television. He had made some modifications to it. He surely must have been the first person in New Zealand to have a remote controlled set.

"It first started," he said, "when the vertical and horizontal hold mechanism went haywire." He had rigged up a number of strings into a harness and series of pulleys. While sitting in his armchair and when the picture revolved horizontally, he would pull on a given string and it would correct itself. If it over corrected he would pull another string to reverse it. There were two more strings for the vertical hold, two for the brightness, two for the volume and a couple of heavy duty ones for the on/off switch. There were two separate strings for the channel changing knob.

So there he'd be every night, sitting in his chair, with about twenty bits of string leading across to the television set. There were only two channels to watch but Dad seemed to have more fun with his remote control system than he did watching the actual TV.

I had been in Alaska just before coming home to visit. Dad's remote control system reminded me of the guys in Anchorage and Fairbanks with their dog sled teams, or a puppeteer at a Punch and Judy show.

I often wondered what would have happened if Mum had pulled the vacuum cleaner out for a rare appearance and if the strings had been sucked up into it. She could have died at fifty-four, not sixty-four!

The Lady Wigram
and The Oxford Reception

Cousin Allan had just come off another remarkable year. He had crashed a couple of cars, had been stung by a million wild bees while clearing bush from his father's farm using a bulldozer and had also made the provincial rugby representative team. These were just a few of the "highlights"!

He had graduated to a Triumph Herald from previous Mark 1 Ford Zephyrs. At 17 years of age, he had crammed a lot into the past two or three of them. Allan would involuntarily convert the Triumph into a convertible a couple of months after a trip to Christchurch. He drove it under a semi-trailer while sailing through an intersection. He said, "I just remembered to duck in time as I steered it between the wheels of the truck. When I came out the other side I had no roof or windows."

Anyway, Allan, my brother Kerry and I decided to drive down to Christchurch for a weekend in January 1966. The reason for the trip was to attend an annual formula one car race called The Lady Wigram Trophy. I had first attended it when I was nine years old and had the privilege of watching Stirling Moss win. I think that was his last race in New Zealand, or anywhere for that matter. He was my hero and I remember reading somewhere in later years that he never managed to obtain a drivers licence. This in spite of the fact that he had sat for the test some twenty-seven times. (So the story went!)

We left Motueka about lunchtime on the Friday and had decided to take the inland route via the Lewis Pass over the Southern Alps. We had barely travelled thirty miles when we stopped on the verge of the country road where a scruffy old bloke we called "Hubcap Harry" was collecting road kill. Scooping it off the road with his shovel and dumping it into a sugar sack, which he carried over his shoulder.

Harry had earned his nickname many years before and was immortalised by Barry Crump, a New Zealand writer of "immortalness" himself. Harry's claim to fame, it is said, was that he could lever off a car's hubcap, insert a dead possum or trout into the hubcap, while carrying on a conversation with the oblivious driver.

Harry reckoned his trick was achieved with much practice with his long handled shovel over many years. He told us initially, he simply pinched the hubcaps and sold them back to the driver at a later stage. This supplemented his unemployment benefit.

I will never know why we stopped, but Allan and Kerry decided to jokingly invite him to join us on our trip. Without even a blink, he threw his bag and his shovel over the fence and piled into the back seat with me. Kerry and Allan just stood in the roadway in absolute shock. After about a quarter of a mile, I was in shock as well and had my head out the window trying to breathe. Hubcap Harry stunk like the local dump!

We discussed putting the smelly old coot in the boot, or better still throwing him into the river from the next bridge. We discussed this aloud and were quite serious about it. Hubcap Harry thought we were joking and he also came up with solutions to the problem, such as tying him to the roof rack for the rest of the journey. He was adamant that he was going to Christchurch with us come hell or high water.

We decided that we would stop at a pub at a place called Springs Junction. Kerry and Allan reckoned that we could get rid of him there by sneaking out of the pub and doing a runner via the dunny's external door. We had it all planned, but when we snuck out the back door of the dunny, Hubcap must have sensed what we were up to. When we arrived at the car, here he was sitting in the back seat. His rightful place!

We drove on at a relentless pace and were approaching the outskirts of Christchurch. At a town called Kaiapoi, Hubcap decided that he had reached his destination. We teased him about having a girlfriend there. He just smiled and bailed out, suggesting that he flag us down on our return on Monday.

"Like hell," we all thought simultaneously!

We drove the rest of the way with all the windows open. It was about six o'clock in the evening when we arrived in Christchurch. Although we had not asked them, we had hoped that we could stay with one of our many uncles and aunties in Christchurch. Perhaps even with our Uncle Hilary and Auntie Nessie in Oxford, a small town north west of Christchurch. Our uncles and aunties provided great refuges for us and always made us welcome.

Before this however I had to contact my new girlfriend Jackie. I had met her during a stint in hospital while exiled to boarding school for a year or so, from Motueka High School.

Anyway, I found a phone and called Jackie who had recently transferred to the Christchurch Public Hospital. She agreed to join us at the car racing the next day. I was so looking forward to seeing her again.

We stayed with Uncle Dan and Auntie Dot that night, after a pub-crawl in Christchurch. We had run into another cousin, Greg, in one of the pubs. He suggested that after the races the next day, we drive to his parents' place in Oxford to taste his home brew. That seemed like a very good idea.

In spite of hangovers, at nine o'clock the next morning we headed for the nurses hostel where Jackie was ensconced. It was great to see her again. We had been writing to each other and I was in love with her (I thought). We had four cartons of beer in the back seat plus the added passenger, Jackie. It was a tight squeeze in the little Triumph. Jackie had to sit up on a carton of beer. The relationship between Jackie and me started going pear shaped from that point on and it had hardly begun!

Kerry didn't help. At one stage, he turned to her and said, "Sitting up there like Jackie." Then he changed to, "Hey Nick, Jackie's sitting up there like a sack of spuds." At this, she burst out crying. Allan had to stop the car so that Jackie and I could get out and I could try to explain Kerry's warped sense of humour and try to calm her down. She didn't stop crying and as she got back into the car, and onto her beer seat, Kerry added, "Hurry up and stop bawling Jackie, we've already missed the first race."

That was the last straw. She cried all the way to the racetrack at Wigram, sobbed for the whole day, and then cried all the way home. Meanwhile Allan thought it was a great joke and I knew damn well that the end was nigh. About two weeks later Jackie wrote me a letter. The content was not that encouraging. My heart was broken for the very first time. Not for long though. Some years later, I heard that Jackie had six kids and was barely thirty years old. Thanks Kerry, you saved me.

After we dropped Jackie off we buggered off to Oxford.

We got there at about seven o'clock that night and Greg welcomed us to Oxford. Auntie Nessie and Uncle Hilary, as usual, were great. After dinner, Greg took us to a local pub where we had more than enough beer. When we arrived home, Greg decided that a nightcap from his stash of home brew was in order. We got right into it, boozing, telling yarns, yelling and whooping and making more noise than a crowd watching the All Blacks beating Australia. We were in Greg's little flat which was about fifty yards away from the farmhouse. About two o'clock in the morning, the door of the flat burst open and Uncle Hilary burst in.

Uncle Hilary was generally a quiet bloke. A real gentleman. He always took time out to listen and could talk to anyone on anyone's level, even ours. Not this morning!

First, he ripped into Greg with a few choice expletives. He even reckoned we had probably woken every farmer in North Canterbury. Greg said, "That's a bit rich Dad," for which he got a swift clip around the ear. I was close to the door and bolted but Uncle Hilary baled Greg, Allan and Kerry up in the flat. I thought they were going to get a belting. But they didn't. Uncle Hilary just ripped into them with a vocabulary only a farmer or a carpenter would know. He was successful in both careers.

I think I slept in the hayshed. I was too scared and too pissed to go back to the house. I doubt if I could have found it anyway!

At breakfast the next morning, Sunday, all four of us sat at the huge kitchen table with the rest of our cousins who also sat in silence. They, unlike us, were eagerly awaiting the consequences. Our manners were very subdued and quietly apologetic for creating such a drunken racket in the early hours of the morning.

Uncle Hilary could not hold himself back any longer. The silence was getting to him and he burst out laughing. This was probably initiated by the small grin on Auntie Nessie's face. She had broken the ice with her favourite saying, "Hilary, boys will be boys you know." And something to the effect that if he did not see the funny side of things then she would tell us some of the things that he, my Dad, and the rest of their brothers got up to when they were our age. Uncle Hilary just grinned and passed around a plate piled high with bacon and eggs.

After that, and up until Uncle Hilary passed away late in 2007, he was always a great bloke to visit. He and Auntie Nessie were sincerely interested in the things their own children, grand children, nephews, and nieces were up to. To me they, like our other Uncles and Aunts, filled the gap left by our Mum and Dad who had passed away so many years before.

Anyway, after breakfast and some hugs and handshakes, a weary Allan, Kerry and I piled into the Triumph and proceeded on the six-hour drive north to Motueka.

Hubcap Harry, the sneaky bugger, was standing on the side of the road on the East Coast Highway just north of the small town called Cheviot, our birthplace. We were sure that we had told him we were returning on Monday via the Lewis Pass, an alternate route, but here he was, flagging us down and it was only Sunday. We decided that maybe we should run him over, but at the last minute, Allan swerved and stopped. Hubcap got his lift home.

Bullfighting In Waiouru, Miller's Acre and The Aussies

The year was 1968. My brother Sean had returned from Australia the previous May and had spent the next few months working in various towns around the country. He was twenty-one years old and had brought a 1967 Chrysler Valiant Wayfarer station wagon back from Australia. He had bought it new off the showroom floor. In those days, it was rare for a twenty-one year old to be driving such a vehicle, let alone own one. Cops often stopped him asking to see ownership papers for the car.

It was the week before Christmas and I joined Sean in Gisborne, a city on the mid-east coast of the North Island. We partied and visited friends, partied and visited more friends, cutting a swathe from coast to coast across the centre of the North Island. We ended up in the city of Rotorua about 8 o'clock on a Saturday morning, all "pubbed" and partied out.

I was a member of the Wellington Skydiving Club and I had brought my parachute with me and decided to make a jump. That afternoon I cadged a ride on a Cessna at Rotorua airport. I was duly given the go ahead to make the jump and was joined by a local jumper. Sean thought I was completely insane jumping from aeroplanes. We made the jump but misjudged the drop zone. My co-jumper landed in a swamp and I landed on the main runway. I was almost bowled by a Fokker Friendship aeroplane as it came in to land. No one told us about that sort of hazard. I can remember visualising the chute being tangled in the propellers and me being rapidly hauled into them and then mince meat! It didn't happen of course but there was a fair amount of yelling and shouting going on as we hurriedly left the airport!

We decided to head back home to the South Island and would make a pit stop in Waiouru, a little town in the centre of the North Island which was also an army base. Our older brother Pat, a Major in the NZ Army, was stationed there.

Being an officer, we knew he would not be living in the actual army barracks but would be with his family in the area set aside for commissioned personnel.

We arrived in Waiouru about midnight. Pat's house was a neat cottage with a three-foot high, neatly trimmed box hedge along the street frontage. We thought it was probably a bit late to wake him. We consumed a half a dozen bottles of beer, discussing our trip to date and telling yarns. We then decided to pitch a tent on his beautifully manicured front lawn. Sean dragged the tent out of the back of the wagon and we proceeded to erect the damn thing.

When you are three parts to the wind, trying to erect a tent in total darkness on someone's front lawn is a bit of a trick. For some unknown reason, I had donned my skydiving helmet, which in those days was much like a motorbike helmet. I was wandering around on the pavement outside the box hedge. Sean held up a red towel and made as if he was a matador. I became the bull. I made a charge, head down straight through the hedge. I tripped and fell flat on my face on the lawn. In the process, I tore a hole in the hedge. Sean jumped the hedge and again taunted the "bull" with the red towel. Back I went, straight through the hedge, missing the matador and the towel and falling on the pavement.

I had about twenty goes at the matador and by this time, the hedge was a trampled mess of leafless stalks and the lawn had great gouges throughout. The racket we were making should have woken the whole army camp. It didn't, and did not even wake brother Pat! So much for national security!

We collapsed into the half-erected tent and awoke to the angry shouting of an army Major. He was threatening some hobos on his front lawn with the military police. He didn't know that the once beautifully manicured front lawn and fence, now in absolute ruin, was the result of a midnight bullfight. The culprits being two of his younger "hobo" brothers!

He calmed down after about an hour and even though the MPs did arrive to cart us off, "The Major" relented and sent them on their way. The sister-in-law was not impressed at all and went into mute mode – just like Mum used to do! She has always looked at me sideways since then. Never forgiving me, I'm sure. The Major (now Colonel retired), often brings up the episode. One we would rather forget.

Sean and I didn't stay long at the Army Base. A couple of longhaired larrikins at such a place was a bit of an embarrassment. Those were the vibes we got anyway. So we made our way down to Wellington, crossed Cook Strait on the inter-island ferry, and finally arrived in the relative sanctuary of Motueka. Just in time for Christmas.

It was now Friday morning and we had to attend Larry Inwood's twenty first birthday party in the Richmond Memorial Hall. It was quite a party and Sean and I, after a bit of gallivanting around visiting some of Sean's old and not so old girlfriends, arrived home the following Tuesday morning. Mum was waiting for us. She was pretty mad and had been since midnight on the previous Friday. She reckoned she was worried sick, not knowing where we were and what we'd been up to. If only she knew! "Just like your father," she said, as she stormed inside the house, retreating into one of her mute modes.

This particular mute mode was cut short by the arrival of three of Sean's Aussie mates, Terry, Billy and Jack from Sydney. Jack was Mum's favourite. He was a giant bloke, a real gentleman, and quiet and reserved. He always called Mum "Mrs Horgan". Most of our mates did. Probably all scared that if they addressed her any other way she would whack them around the ears. She had that sort of "Mrs look" about her.

It was now Tuesday evening and New Year's Eve and we were off to the city of Nelson, some thirty miles away for a party not to be missed. It was a tradition that every New Year's Eve, there would be a huge party in the centre of the city held at a venue called Miller's Acre. This was simply a large tar sealed car park, diagonally opposite the Post Office. Crowds poured out of the pubs leading up to midnight. When the clock in the tower above the Post Office struck midnight everyone went crazy, running around and kissing every one else. In hindsight it was quite bizarre. Sean had parked the Valiant in the centre of Miller's Acre. The tailgate was down and inside the car we had oodles of beer. We were either sitting on the tailgate or on the ground drinking beer and taking in the wild scene.

"We," consisted of Sean, Kerry, Jack, Terry, Billy, the odd girlfriend or two and me. A complete stranger from Christchurch, we were later to find out, made his way to the car and swiped a couple of bottles of beer. Kerry decided that this was not on and sent out a wild haymaker. Kerry was doing quite well fighting not only the bloke from Christchurch, but also a couple of his mates. Then things went pear-shaped for Kerry, and he was getting a bit of a hiding. Sean and the rest of us were still sitting, egging Kerry on, but taking no part in the brawl. They had Kerry down on the deck and were about to put the boot in. Jack, the gentle, mild mannered giant, decided something ought to be done to even up the odds a bit. He walked into the mêlée and before he could even get a bit of the action, he slipped and fell on his bum.

At the exact same time, the cops arrived with a paddy wagon and a police dog. They grabbed poor old Jack and threw him into the back of the wagon, along with the bloke from Christchurch. The bloke from Christchurch had a girlfriend with him. She decided that the cops were not going to have her man and waded into the action. We still sat on the back of the station wagon's tailgate, clapping and cheering.

Then things went from bad to worse and "worse to worser!" The girlfriend bit the police dog! We all bolted and mingled into the crowd, egging the now angry Alsatian on. It was taking chunks out of the girlfriend at an alarming rate. The cops hauled the dog off the girlfriend and threw her into the paddy wagon as well.

The scene quietened down a bit after the cops drove the wagon away. We followed it to the police station to try to explain that Jack, now in custody, had nothing to do with the fight. The cops didn't want to know and threw us out of the station, telling us to meet Jack at the courthouse the next morning at ten o'clock or join him for the night.

We arrived home at 4 o'clock in the morning. You guessed it. Mum was waiting for us. She really ripped into us when she discovered that her favourite Aussie, Jack, was in jail.

At ten o'clock, New Year's Day, we arrived at the courthouse. Jack was given bail and the case was set for a hearing in a couple of weeks' time. We took Jack straight to the airport, where he flew to Wellington and then on to Sydney the same day, never to return to New Zealand.

Again, we got a lambasting from the "Old Lady" when we arrived back home without her favourite Aussie. We told her that he had to get home to Sydney for "family reasons". How anyone could have a favourite Aussie sure amused me.

Lunch (The Following Year)

As usual, it had been a tough New Year's Eve. We had decided to give Miller's Acre a miss this year and had held our own party. Now, at 5 a.m on New Year's Day all the players who'd been stayers were starting to succumb to slumber.

We were sprawled around the lounge room of Tony Wing's house in Motueka. His place had those old wooden sashed windows, which slid up and down in tracks using pulleys and a lightweight rope. The morning was already hot and the windows had been pushed up and open.

Two roosters crowed a raucous crow somewhere close by in the neighbourhood. They knew by instinct that this was the time for the wake up call but no one told them that this day was not the day to do it! This morning of all mornings, humans needed sleep.

The only one who heeded the roosters' call was Tony. He stumbled through the open window and found the concrete path outside with his head. No problems there as his head had received far worse treatment over the years. A few minutes later, both roosters sailed through the window, necks wrung and all out of crow.

"Lunch," said Tony.

The Good Ship Aramoana

The open sea passage between the North and the South Islands of New Zealand is known as Cook Strait. It is where the Tasman Sea meets the Pacific Ocean and can be a violent stretch of water. Many ships have come to grief, perhaps the worst was the *Wahine*, which capsized in the late '60s with great loss of life.

As a matter of interest, in 2008 somebody swam across the strait in a record time of four hours. The previous record, if I recall, was thirteen hours.

The actual distance between the two islands is only thirteen nautical miles. Ferries run between the two islands departing from Wellington in the North Island and Picton in the South Island. Wellington is virtually on the southern tip of the North Island but Picton is some twenty-seven miles into the Marlborough Sounds at the top of the South Island. Thus, the ferry trip is about a total distance of forty miles and takes about four hours.

In the late 1950s the Government introduced a new inter-island ferry. A ship designed to carry heaps of cars, trains and people. It would eventually ply the route from Wellington to Picton, back and forth all day every day. The ship was named "*Aramoana*".

It was not a small boat and could carry 200-300 cars, a couple of trains and their full wagons plus hundreds of passengers. It was called a "roll on roll off" system. You did exactly that, just drove straight onto the ship into either one of the two vehicle decks. Above these decks were another two or three decks with restaurants, lounges and a bar.

The *Armoana* was such a success that by 1969 there were three such ships and I believe there are now four, even bigger ones.

My brothers Sean, Kerry, a friend Jim Carman, our cousin Allan and I headed off to Wellington on the 3rd of January 1969. Kerry and I were off to work in Wellington and the others off to Australia. This was an annual pilgrimage for Sean, racing around after the big money that could be earned in Australia compared to New Zealand at the time. You had to be prepared to work bloody hard for it though.

The sailing ship we were booked on was due to leave at eleven p.m. and so a pub-crawl from Motueka to Picton seemed a fair bet. In addition to the pubs in the towns of Motueka, Richmond, Nelson and Blenheim en-route to Picton there were nine wayside inns. Each one received a visit from us that afternoon!

We duly "rolled" on to the ferry at 10:45 p.m. in Sean's car but to our dismay found that the ship's bar was closed because of a ten p.m. curfew. Just as well we had our own supplies of beer stashed in Allan's cricket bag in the car.

It was just after the Christmas-New Year holiday so the ship was crowded. People were everywhere and any sort of seat was at a premium. It was as hot as hell in spite of the midnight voyage. We finally found ourselves a spot on the top deck in an area out of bounds to the public. It was amongst coils of rope and chains and other "ship's stuff". As the ship sailed off, Sean, Kerry and I sat on the coils of rope. Allan had gone to the car on a deck far below to fetch the beer in his cricket bag. Jimmy had found a comfortable seat, with air conditioning, elsewhere in the main lounge.

As we sat, we heard muffled voices coming from somewhere close by. We traced the voices to a sea chest some ten feet from where we were sitting. The chest was a wooden box about six feet long, three feet wide and three feet high. From what we could gather, tonight it held a bloke and what we thought was his girlfriend.

We pretended to be deck hands, giving orders to lock up all the sea chests and securing lose fittings. Then we quickly sat on the lid of the box trying to figure a way to secure it. The bloke in the box panicked and got a bit "emotional" I suppose you could say. His girlfriend was screaming and now we were in a bit of strife ourselves.

The bloke in the box, we decided to call him "Jack," was trying to push the lid up and open. He would get it up a few inches and then, with our weight on it, it would bang down again. He must have rolled onto his back and pushed up with his feet because he seemed to get a bit stronger with each progressive lift. Things were hotting up so we told Jack that we were going to tie the box up and throw it overboard if he didn't calm down a bit.

This seemed to make him madder. It was about then that we realised that we were the ones that were trapped. Jack was threatening us with all sorts of weird endings and he was getting more leverage with each lift. He was almost to the stage where his next lift would fling us off the lid. Jack would force the lid up about a foot and, crash, it would bang down again.

Where the hell was Allan when you needed him! We urgently required some rope to tie the lid down but it was out of reach. None of us could get off the lid to get the rope because with less weight on top Jack would then be able to open it. Now what we needed somewhat more than urgently, was an escape plan.

We decided that the next time the lid crashed down, Sean would count to three and we would all make a run for the stairs. They had not played that trick on me for years and I had forgotten that they would bolt on the count of two!

They did and on the count of "three", Jack, in the box, tried the lid.

Being the only one left on the lid as Jack booted it up, I did a backward flip over the box and landed in a big coil of rope. This saved me from going through the railing and down eighty feet into the sea below. Thank God it was dark up there.

It was all happening at once.

Sean and Kerry hit the top of the stairs, which were about twenty feet high and bloody steep. Halfway down the stairs, they hit Allan coming up with the bag of beer and they all tumbled to the deck below. I guess the booze in them prevented any injuries but all the bottles in the bag broke.

Jack was now out of the box and was dragging his girlfriend out after him. He was shouting threats and abuse at his unknown pranksters and trying to get accustomed to what little light there was. I was shitting myself, as I was only about ten feet from him. I had been lucky not to go over the side of the ship but Jack's mood told me that if he saw me I'd be over the side anyway!

Jack's girlfriend saved me. She insisted that Jack take her back to her husband below decks immediately or she would tell him that Jack had been a naughty boy with his best mate's wife!

An hour later, we were driving off the ferry and telling Jimmy the story. He had one to tell us as well.

He said that while he was sitting in the main lounge area along with another 200 to 300 other people, the whole room quickly filled with a misty fog. The fog had mysteriously disappeared after a few minutes. This had happened five or six times during the trip. We did not think much about it at the time but the next day we were again discussing the ferry trip and how we had spent most of it in the "out of bounds" area.

While in the "out of bounds" area we had to relieve ourselves, a result of the earlier pub-crawl. We had peed into the intake grills of what we thought were some bloody great generators. There was no dunny up there. It then dawned on us that the "bloody great generators" were air-conditioners, air intakes, or evaporative coolers of some sort. Hence the fine mist in the lounges below. I am unsure as to how this could happen, or even if it did, but it is the only explanation we had.

I hope Jimmy never reads this!

Acting The Goat. Literally.

My brother Kerry's 21st birthday was a great night. In the early hours of the next morning, Mum again went into her famous mute mode when she woke up to a commotion going on in the lounge room.

There Kerry and his hangmen mates were riding a couple of goats around the room. They had "borrowed" them from around the neighbourhood. Some local farmers had the habit of chaining goats to steel posts on the grass verges of the streets bordering their properties. Saved cutting the grass I guess. Dad was sitting in his favourite chair with his banjo playing and singing "*Paddy McGinty's goat*".

The grit well and truly hit the fan when around eight o'clock the next morning, the local traffic cop, who had parked his "black and white" outside his house, just four houses up the street from us, found four goats in his patrol car!

They had peed, poo'd, and eaten the leather seats, his brief case and paperwork, as well as his tunic. The inside of the car was in write-off condition. No one was ever caught for this stunt, but the local police "had their suspicions!" It was rumoured that the culprit took off to Australia later that afternoon.

Many years later I heard that this stunt was performed by some kids who weren't even born when Kerry and his mates were "alleged" to have done it in the early '70s. I'm sure they can have the credit for it however, as far as Kerry is concerned!

The Dunedin Trio and "Woodstock Australian Style"

Shepparton, Australia. 1969

Sid, Marty and Daryl were from Dunedin in New Zealand's South Island. They had arrived in Shepparton, Australia for the fruit-picking season. The same year I decided to join my brother Sean in Shepparton as well. He had been picking fruit there since about 1965. Shepparton is about three hours drive from Melbourne. It would be my first and last season there, as I was not cut out for picking pears in forty-degree heat. Jimmy Carman, our mate from Motueka, was also there that year.

It was the time the world had gone haywire with hippies and rock festivals all over the show, the most famous of all being *Woodstock* in the USA. One of Australia's equivalents, *The Miracle*, was scheduled to be held at Launching Place, a tiny town in the hills about an hour out of Melbourne. I guess the event was called *The Miracle* due to its being held at Easter and the raising of the dead, etc. At least that seemed appropriate to some heathen hippie. It was to be held over the four day holiday and most of Australia's rock bands of the time would be there. So would Marty, Sid, Daryl, Jimmy and I. We left Shepparton after lunch on Good Friday travelling in Marty's 1961 Holden, "with a 1968 motor in it," he liked to inform everyone.

With our long-haired heads sticking out of ponchos made of coloured blankets we arrived at Launching Place. The organisers of the festival had certainly chosen a great spot. The hills surrounded a flat paddock of four or five acres. A natural amphitheatre. Thousands of people were arriving on the Friday evening for the Saturday morning kick-off. Hippies and yippies pitched their tents on the gentle slopes of the hills overlooking the site.

We froze that evening. Our tent was tied to a tree at one end, and to a single pole at the other end. I had discovered that the big gum tree acting as one of the poles had a hollowed out base. Just like a big open fireplace. I decided to use it as exactly that and lit a fire in the hollow tree trunk's base. The fire really warmed us up and we sat drinking beer, looking down at the preparations taking place below us for the big three days to come.

After about half an hour, a couple of people down in the amphitheatre below started to wave up at us. We waved back. Then more people were looking up in our direction, pointing and waving. We kept waving back and boozing on until half a dozen security men began running up the hill.

"Something's up somewhere," said Jimmy. It sure was! The tree where I had built my fire was about a hundred feet high and at the fifty foot mark there was a hole, just like a chimney. Flames and smoke were pouring out of the hole, in fact the whole tree was on fire. Shit, we all grabbed our bedrolls and beer and bolted, trying desperately to merge into the huge crowd gathering below and about us.

There was no water anywhere near the place and the fire burnt on and on. A miracle all right. It was a bloody miracle I didn't start a massive forest fire. Aussies are pretty hot to trot about that. The security people were tearing around trying the find the firelighters. Jimmy Carman was screaming out, "His name is Hogan (without the R) and he's not with us." Getting right into the festive mood, I was repeating what Jimmy was saying and trying to find the culprit as well.

Finally, the fire department arrived but not before a severe rainstorm hit the venue and put the fire out. It rained all night and into the next day. The "Miracle Hippie Happening" was cancelled and we drove sombre but not sober, back to Shepparton.

The next day the front page of the Saturday papers in Melbourne featured a photo of the blazing tree. In the photo, Jimmy and I had our backs to the camera, pointing at the fire!

Anyway, we had arrived back in Shepparton on the Saturday evening and decided to go to the pub. A jug of beer was one dollar. From the jugs, we filled our glasses. The pub closed at midnight. Sid, of the Dunedin trio, was an absolute guts. He'd eat or drink anything not nailed down. Sean had filled seven glasses from the beer that remained in the last jugs of the evening. There were six of us in our group. I had gone to take a leak and when I returned, I had with me one of the little blue tablets they put in urinals to tone down the odour. Sid was hurriedly finishing his drink with one eye on the seventh and last beer, left standing on the table. He quickly gulped down his beer and grabbed for the seventh glass taking a small sip to claim it. I slid the tablet from my pocket and while Sean distracted Sid, I dropped the tablet in the glass!

The beer reared up and fizzed all over the table. Jimmy was trying to brush the froth away so that Sid didn't see it, but the beer kept bubbling over. So Sean said, "We're out of here." We grabbed our almost finished beers, gulped them down and started to walk from the pub. Poor old Sid had to gulp down nearly a full middy of frothy beer. There was no way he was going to waste it.

We left the pub in Marty's 1961/1968 Holden and drove out of the town to our accommodation. We were working on a farm owned by the

Turnbull Brothers who employed thirty to forty pickers. Our lodgings consisted either of separate individual bunkhouses or rooms in the converted original Turnbull homestead. The two-storeyed homestead had a verandah along one side on the upper level. Four stout posts supported the verandah and Marty used the area underneath to park his 1961/68 Holden.

The driveway into the Turnbull farm was straight for about half a mile before turning ninety degrees left, then ninety degrees right. At the speed Marty was travelling that night there was no way he was going to make the first bend and the car, with wheels on full lock, kept going straight ahead. The car left the road and headed out onto a half an acre of mown lawn. It was a frosty night and although Marty was standing on the brakes, the car kept up its speed of around 60 miles an hour. We left the mown lawn and headed directly for the homestead. "Wonder where Ross Turnbull wants a new door!" yelled Sean. Marty managed to miss the house proper but took out three of the four veranda posts. We came to a grinding halt up against the fourth post. Before we could bale out, the complete second storey verandah crashed down on us!

The next morning after a few hours sleep, we gathered in the pre-work day mustering area. Here Ross Turnbull would address the crews and direct them to the areas that needed picking. He had his back to the old homestead. All the pickers were laughing their heads off at the sight behind Ross. The 1961/68 Holden sat mangled under the pile of what used to be the veranda. Ross couldn't figure why we were all laughing and said something to the effect that picking fruit was a serious matter. How critical it was to keep the stalks on the fruit and not bruise them and that it was not a laughing matter. We all bolted on the tractors and carts, leaving Ross scratching his head and wondering what the hell was going on.

I still can't fathom why he didn't see the funny side of it the next morning when he addressed us once more. Marty wasn't at the briefing that morning. Neither was Sid. He had some very serious illness and was in hospital where he almost died!

Alexander Patrick Horgan

"A man much loved by his family and admired and respected by all who knew him, but none more than I"

There were many things we wanted to do or try when we were youngsters. Dad would never say "No". Instead, he would simply say, "I tried it when I was your age. It didn't work for me but it might for you." We thought twice.

This was a shrewd way of making us think very seriously before we tried various stunts. He knew damn well that if he said no, then we would go and do it anyway. If he said yes we would still do it, and if it went wrong we would blame him! Most of the time, however, there was no way we were going to confide our next stunt and most of them were not premeditated anyway.

He was only five foot six but he was a tough, strong little bloke. He had a heart of gold and a wonderful and generous nature. He was always whistling a tune. A popular man who had no enemies and his people skills were exceptional. He excelled in all sports and as a young man represented his country in a couple of them.

He fought for his country in Europe in the early 1940s. In Italy, he exchanged two tins of sardines and four packets of smokes for a German prisoner of war's Iron Cross. He was the sort of bloke who would never steal. For the German it was a fair exchange, "You can't eat an Iron Cross."

His only, and legendary statement from his tour of duty was, "I carried this damned 303 Lee Enfield rifle up and down Italy four times and never ever fired a shot." I never believed that statement! Strangely enough, he still had the old Lee Enfield in his wardrobe. I never thought to ask how he had managed to keep it and often wonder what ever happened to it.

Dad returned to New Zealand in 1945 to get on with life. It was as if his years in Europe were a training ground for the next few years of being around when Mum brought up the seven children! The stress for both Dad and Mum during our childhood years was possibly worse than during the years he spent away at the war.

Trout fishing was his greatest outside interest and he was the "master fisherman", his patience being the key. He was one of the few people who would set his net for whitebait and then walk the river with his rod, casting for trout. With his whitebait net over his shoulder, a haversack on his back, Sean under one arm, Kerry under the other, and me on his shoulders holding his trout rod, I still recall him wading across Moon Creek, up to his waist in water. We were four, five and six years old. His *"Three Small Suspects"*.

He played the banjo mandolin, the violin and the piano and he could take his bow and play a tune on a handsaw from the garage. He was better at this last stunt after he had consumed a few warm beers. He would let us have a sip or two as well.

The banjo mandolin went most places he did and he would play, laugh, and sing. His eyes would crinkle at the sides with sheer enjoyment and happiness. His favourite songs were Irish and he knew and sang them all in tune while he played his music on his banjo mandolin.

The Banjo Mandolin

Unplayed since nineteen seventy-four
Now it leans against the wall
Beneath his photo pride of place
Just along from the fireplace
It never played a crooked note
Had travelled cross the sea by boat
From thirty-nine to forty-three
To Middle East and Italy
My memories are very plain
On this pair our eyes were trained
The man it 'owned' for fifty years
It brought much laughter, never tears
Five under five and two pre-war
And the children from next door
Would sit and listen to the strings
Learning all the songs he'd sing
And Dad would play with silly grin
So many songs were known to him
The Irish songs like 'Golden Slippers'
Or classical and little ditties
I'd look at Mum, she was so proud
Of Father and his little crowd
Yes, it was his pride and joy
When I was just a little boy

James Nicholas
August 1983

The Wake

Getting Dad to visit a doctor was like trying to get turkeys to endorse Thanksgiving and Christmas.

His cancer was diagnosed way too late and at the age of sixty-four, he passed away. Far too young. He had probably had the dreaded disease for years but during the last two years of his life, the deterioration was very noticeable. Through all this he suffered in silence, refusing to see a doctor until just a few weeks before he died. This visit put him directly into hospital, never to go home again. He never complained or blamed anything, such as tobacco, which was probably the cause.

Only Mum, my sister Veronica and I were in New Zealand at the time of his death. We had to wait for over a week for the other members of the family to come home from places like the USA, Australia, the UK, Thailand and Singapore. At the mortuary his four sons sat and told jokes as if he was sitting there with us and laughing at our silly lines, in pure Irish tradition.

It was a sad and frustrating time. The funeral seemed to be attended by everyone in the district, as his popularity was enormous. His four sons and their friends needed a release valve. However, more than air would be expelled from the valves that night.

One of Dad's favourite sayings when a guess turned out to be correct or when something was better than good, was "Bang on!"

The wake, held at home, was a beaut and at midnight, we decided that more food was required. As usual, I drew the short straw and was sent to scour the town for some grub.

Fetching food at midnight in Motueka in 1977 was no easy feat. The only place open was the pie cart on the corner of the town's main intersection of High and Greenwood Streets. It was a mobile caravan constructed of plywood over a steel frame with a metal roof and a canvas awning. Towed by a panel van, the owner used to park it on the same spot every afternoon until the early hours of the following morning, six days a week. It had recently been sold to a bloke called Squelch. I never knew what his real name was and didn't really care because he was a bit of a dipstick.

My brother-in-law, Jim, a Yank, decided that he would join me in my search for food and we duly arrived at the pie cart. Jim and I were the only customers at the time and I ordered a large amount of fish and chips, oysters and scallops. Squelch only had one scallop left but he fried it up anyway. He then proceeded to ask fifty cents for the single miserable scallop. I told him that I would give him twenty cents or nothing to which he replied, "Nothing." So I said thanks, grabbed the scallop, and ate it!

Squelch had actually meant that "nothing" meant no deal. He got a bit upset at my deliberate misinterpretation and jumped the serving counter of the mobile pie cart threatening to slap me around a bit. Jim came to the rescue and after a lengthy argument on the price of scallops he paid for the fish and chips with American dollars. Squelch was happy with that but I wasn't and told him so. With this, he decided to have another spar with me but Jim bundled me into the car and we drove home.

I related the story to my brothers and their friends when Jim and I returned to the wake. A lengthy debate began on whether or not Squelch needed to "get his" — whether or not the younger brother needed defending.

About 1.30 a.m., I developed a combination of severe migraine and drunkenness and decided to find a bedroom in which to sleep it off. At 3.30 a.m., a hellish explosion awakened the whole township. At 6 a.m., there was a banging and crashing on the front door of our home. A hung-over voice shouted from somewhere telling whoever it was to bugger off and come back at a reasonable hour, like mid-day. The banging continued until someone else decided to investigate only to find that the entire Motueka police force, comprising two constables and a sergeant, was on the front verandah.

The cops demanded the whereabouts of certain members of the Horgan family and their friends. The inference was that these blokes had allegedly blown up the local pie cart in the early hours of the morning. One of the cops said that they had already caught one of the alleged offenders and that he was in jail. They also reckoned that someone may have been killed but as the pie cart was now a pile of embers, they could not find him or her. Scorched fish and chips supposedly covered an area in the middle of the town for about two hundred yards in every direction.

The story circulating around the town was that a group of yet unidentified youths in their late teens and early twenties had done the deed. That they had used massive quantities of explosives such as dynamite, gelignite, thunder flashes and detonators to blow up the pie cart. This was reportedly an act of retribution for an earlier altercation at the now basically "vacant" site.

The facts were liberally embellished with conjecture and imagination over the ensuing days. The possible beginnings of Al Qaeda. Three suspects had been questioned by police and released pending an enquiry.

The three were later charged with bombing the pie cart. A date was set for the hearing.

After a week or so things settled down a bit and almost got off the front pages of the *Christchurch Press*, *Wellington's Dominion* and the *Nelson Evening Mail*. The Press had the last word when it reported, "Bang on joke ends in court". Dad would have just loved that. A fitting send off. The wording was more than a bit of a coincidence but we let it lie. I have often wondered who the person was who offered the headline to the Press. It must have been someone who knew Dad pretty well.

The story up to when Jim and I got back home from the pie cart is true. The rest is surmised as follows:

Some of our friends were fishermen who trawled Tasman Bay. It was rumoured that many of these ships had flares, thunder flashes, detonators, and some supposedly had a little stash of gelignite. These devices were reputedly used to stun the odd shoal of fish or for other dubious or competitive reasons.

The pie cart had a small area at one end where half a dozen people could sit around an oval table and eat a steak and egg meal or whatever they ordered from the menu. The rest of the pie cart consisted of the cooking galley, which included a couple of large deep frying vats, a series of hot plates and a small kitchen area.

All of this was open plan and if you were the cook or the owner in this case, standing inside the pie cart, you would look out over a counter or servery. The customers would enter under a canvas walled awning. They could buy takeaway food, stand and drink coffee, or eat a meal from off the counter if the dining part of the pie cart was full.

The canvas awning covered an area about thirty feet in length and extended halfway out over the footpath. At the opposite end of the pie cart from the dining area, a door led out to the van which towed the pie cart. The van also stored the uncooked and precooked food.

The servery or counter was a couple of feet wide and about twenty feet long. It was alleged that the perpetrators had placed a ten-gallon drum of water under the counter in the gutter of the street.

Supposedly, there were four so-called bombers, one of whom stayed with the car across the street in readiness for a quick getaway.

Three young men stood at the counter and ordered coffee, shielding the drum of water with their lower bodies from prying eyes. One of the youths was believed to have dropped some thunder flashes and the odd detonator into the drum and all three bolted. They got to the car and nothing happened. So they walked back to give the water a "further priming", with what is anyone's guess, and again they took off to the car.

The explosion, which one could have been reasonably proud of, caused the driver to stall the getaway car. The perpetrators were last seen by an anonymous taxi driver, trying to push start the car.

A bang and a bit of water splashed around the pie cart was all that was intended. But the double dose of accelerant, which rumour had exaggerated to become C4, had totally annihilated the pie cart.

The water in the can was actually the real culprit! It flew up out of the drum; hit the underside of the counter and shot off at an angle to the ceiling of the awning. From there it was deflected at right angles directly into the boiling vats of oil and onto the hot plates. Water, boiling fat and gas cook tops don't seem to mix that well. Kind of like spraying water on a petrol fire.

The second explosion, a muffled thump, was probably an implosion. Confining itself to the inside of the pie cart until the walls and roof ran out of air and then the whole thing disintegrated. There was no-one in the pie cart at the time in spite of a rumour that a young Maori bloke was missing. His package of fish and chips was etched into the now blistered paint of Manoy's bottle shop fence. No body, no problem!

The canvas awning burnt for a while and the overall heat of the fire cooked any remaining fish and chips in the wreckage of the pie cart.

Squelch himself was reasonably lucky as he had gone out the door of the pie cart and into the van to fetch some more supplies. He was still in the refrigerated van when the whole kit and caboodle went up.

No one ever managed to locate the mystery Maori boy or any remains of him. Somewhere in New Zealand there is probably a deaf, elderly Maori wandering around still wondering what the hell was on the fish and chips he bought in a pie cart in Motueka some thirty years ago!

The courtroom was packed for Squelch versus the rest of the world. Secretly, it seemed, even the police were on the defendants' side, along with the judge and the lawyers for both parties. This was possibly because Squelch was a prick!

The only unhappy, but confident court attendee was Squelch. He was certain that he would get full compensation and that the perpetrators would get the nine year jail term, as indicated by law. The miserable bastard was probably not insured. He also had no sense of humour and hoped that these bloody little terrorists would finally get what was due to them, for twenty-five years of pranks around the town.

On the perpetrators' behalf, had it not been for a taxi driver who had no respect for Dad, the case would never have got to court.

When the Police Sergeant produced "Exhibit A," the only evidence, the whole courtroom erupted in laughter, and so did the Sergeant. The judge tried desperately to keep a straight face as well. It was a fun story after all and no one was hurt. Put the town of Motueka on the map – or almost took it off!

"Exhibit A", the only exhibit, was a crumpled ten-gallon drum supposedly found some two hundred yards from the scene. "Could have been a water can from any one of a thousand back yards or origins," said the defence lawyer. The judge nodded and turned and looked the defendants straight in the eye and said, "But it wasn't, was it boys?"

The boys allegedly got a nine month suspended sentence and a forty dollar fine between the lot of them.

Postscript

A friend of Dad's was a bloke called Ron Macintosh. He was a barman at the Post Office Hotel at the time. Sean, Kerry and I returned home to Motueka some months after the so-called bombing. We decided to pop into the Post Office Hotel for a quiet beer. As we entered, the pub was crowded and from behind the bar, Ron Mac yelled, "Everybody duck, the bombers are back in town".

The whole bar except Ron, Sean, Kerry and me, dived to the floor.

We didn't buy a beer that night. Many of the patrons were Dad's mates. They insisted on buying us beers and reminding us of all the good times, they had with Dad and his banjo mandolin, his laughter and yarns and especially his generosity. There were also people who came up to us wanting to pay back pub loans that Dad had given them when they were short. Loans that would never be repaid due to the untimely death of Alexander Patrick Horgan. Loans that his sons would never claim either.

Mum's Mini

Dad was a sincere believer that only men should drive motor cars. Over the years, debate on this topic was repeatedly rekindled. Sometimes it almost got to the voting stage around the dinner table. We kids thought we knew damn well that Dad's much recited simile of Mum driving would be like "a pig with a shilling", was probably correct and so the ruling party stayed in power.

Each time Mum conceded and continued to ride her bike and even on that, she was like a pig with a shilling!

Dad passed away in 1977 and the second thing on Mum's agenda after she had chucked the old man into a hole, was to buy herself a car. We all had our doubts about this. I even thought she might have wanted to join Dad a bit sooner than she had planned.

There was no way that any of her kids were going to even think about giving her driving lessons. We doubted that anyone else in the town would have the patience either. Anyway, someone did and she got her licence. With her newfound freedom and independence she would drive around all over the place, visiting people and carting around her flowers.

One evening she decided to drive and spend the evening with my sister in Nelson, a city some thirty miles away. The first ten miles of the journey is along a highway, which is a series of causeways around the coast of part of Tasman Bay. Concrete pipes under the road ensure that the tidal water flows into and out of the little lakes formed by the causeways.

The road was reasonably straight and had long, easy to navigate bends, as opposed to the twisting winding gravel road it used to be. About midnight Mum was returning home and approximately five miles from home, she ran off the road. No one knows what happened or how she managed to do this. Maybe she fell asleep.

Anyway, her little Morris Mini left the road and landed about ten feet below the level of the road and twenty yards out into one of the little lakes. The car landed on the water on all four wheels and slowly started to sink. The tide was in. Mum was in a bit of strife! There was no other traffic on the highway and even if there had been, her car would not have been visible from the road.

About five hundred yards away in a house on a hill top, a farmer had been up watching some late night TV. On his way to bed, he had just turned the lights out in the lounge. For some reason he looked out of the lounge window into the darkness. His house overlooked the little lake, over the causeway and out into Tasman Bay. The daytime view was magnificent but in darkness, it was exactly that: dark.

However, the view this night was different. The glow of two lights under the water in the causeway lake was probably something he would never see again. Curiosity moved him to investigate further. He strolled outside into the cold night air of early September and to his astonishment, there below him was a car in the lake with its headlights blazing.

He ran down to the lake, waded in, dived down, wrenched the door open and dragged a sodden Jan Horgan out of the car and out of the water to safety.

Mum never talked about it much even when we all joked with her about it. I do remember however, her muttering something a few weeks after she got her reconditioned mini back. She was mimicking Dad's words about her driving a car would be like "a pig with a shilling" and silently she pursed her lips as if she was set to move into her famous mute mode.

She changed her mind on the mute mode thing, opened the car door, sat in the driver's seat, fired it up and set off to Nelson to prove the old man wrong. Rumour has it however, that she drove to Nelson and back via the alternative inland route.

Charlotte Jeanne Horgan (nee Falkinder)

Mum was born in 1918 in a town called Little River, on the Canterbury Peninsula, New Zealand. She didn't speak to us much about her childhood, at least not to me.

Her loves were flowers, cooking and family and she coped adequately with all three. She specialised in growing and showing gladioli and boasted an individually named collection of some 10,000 different varieties. She knew the names of each of them by sight, which was a trick in itself. Mum was always on the scrounge for empty blocks of land in which she could plant her glads and Pat and Peter Goodman let her use a quarter acre block adjacent to their bakery. In summer, it was a blaze of colour.

As a matter of interest, Mum died at the relatively young age of sixty-four and in hindsight, I have wondered if it was the glads that killed her. Not the flowers themselves but the poisons, such as the Derris Dust she used to preserve the cormlets. She never wore gloves or a mask when she used these products and her health was up and down like a whore's drawers.

She had dedicated one of her hybrid "glads" to each of her children. Mine she named Pilot and it had an off-white coloured flower with a purple throat. I often wondered if it was "Pontius" Pilate but I was never game enough to ask. If you went to a Catholic school, you soon learned that Pontius was the name of a really bad bugger a couple of thousand years before who had allegedly given the nod for Christ's crucifixion. I have never known a Catholic kid named Pontius, or any other kid for that matter and I can understand why. As for his surname, Pilate, I was always under the impression it was spelled "Pilot" and the only pilots I knew at the time were *Biggles* and Graeme Bond, a neighbour down the street from us. My train of thought at the time, while sitting in Sister Gabriel's catechism class, was of this bloke called Pontious "Pilot" flying around Jerusalem a couple of thousand years ago in a Tiger Moth!

Kerry's glad was Firebrand, a deep red. Sean's was Pinocchio. It was a miniature and a motley orange, blotchy brown colour. This was probably because Sean had heaps of little brown freckles when he was young. I can't remember the names Mum had allocated to the glads she had dedicated to the rest of the family but can think of some in hindsight that would have fitted perfectly!

Mum had a great sense of humour and used to tell the odd yarn or two. She never ever used a swear word or crude expression of any kind. I was quite shocked one day however, when she told us the story of a little incident that happened when Dad was away at the War. Mum was living in the small town of Cheviot in North Canterbury. She had two young children, Pat and Hilary, at the time and like most mothers, whose husbands were away at the war, found it pretty tough going.

She had a push mower and would mow the lawns in the front of the house every week or two. Often, she said, a little old bloke would walk past the front gate and try to engage in conversation. He had a speech impediment and every now and again, he would reverse the first letters of every noun he used. His favourite saying was "How is your mawn lower going Mrs

Horgan?" Yet when he strung together a long sentence there was no sign of the mixing of letters. One day, they were in conversation, most of it being Mum's, discussing hardships of the war years. Of how the women left at home had to perform a myriad of tasks that their husbands would normally have done. The little old man piped up and said, "When my father was away at the First World War, my 'old lady' had to do all sorts of tasks on our farm. She could do five things at once. She could talk and knit, carry the kit, fart and drive the pigs to market!"

I laughed when Mum told us that story and have always remembered it. Not only was it funny to us littlies at the time but it was so out of character for Mum to use such a crude word.

In September 1982, on a beautiful spring evening I had a call from a neighbour to come home from work urgently. I found Mum lying in her gladioli garden. She called it her "plot". She had passed away amongst her flowers as she always said she would. The odds of that happening were high simply because she was nearly always in her flower garden.

She lay beside a row of seven freshly planted "corms" or young gladioli seedlings, which she had obviously planted within the last hour of her life. Each of the corms had a cut down white Venetian blind strip pushed into the ground beside it. Written on each marker was the name of the "glad" she had dedicated to each of her children. It was as if she knew that her time had come and she had done this and then lay down to take a rest. At each end of the small row, she had planted forget-me-nots! It seemed to be a reminder for us to plant the same flowers on her grave. That was a promise she never needed to coerce us into making some years before.

I will always remember that afternoon. She could not have picked a better one. I sat beside her in the garden, wishing that I had spent more quality time with her. Wishing that I had treated her better than I had and wishing for so many things that would have made her life so much better. Mum however, would not have wanted to change her life for anything other than the one she had lived.

Mother

A year today she went away
She left us sad like father had
Through years of hardship and of toil
She seemed so peaceful on the soil
'mid flowers and earth her heart did stop
No better place, she called her 'plot'
Her family scattered 'round the globe
All seven came in hours to home
'No better place' she'd often said
To go to God from her flower bed
T'was if he'd heard her joyful plea
A warm spring evening just on tea
And now I speak for friends and kin
Without a hint of selfish whim
You were so good and kind to us
And never really made a fuss
When things went wrong, against the grain
You didn't seem to feel the pain
Four fine sons and three fair daughters
'God was kind' I heard her whisper
To father once when I was there
He winked his eye 'A fine brood mare'
This I'm sure I heard replied
And tears of happiness she cried
Her time had come to be at rest
For all of us she'd done her best
I'll for one for life remember
That warm spring evening in September
Dad had gone five years before
And they were both just sixty four

James Nicholas
September 1983

KERRY   NICK   SEAN

Snippets

Crisp's Garage

Mr Crisp, next door, owned a local milk bar and tearooms. His name was Jack and funnily enough, he stocked *Frosty Jack* ice cream, which I thought was interesting. He had a huge chest freezer in his garage where he used to keep his excess ice cream and he'd take it pack by pack to work each day, as he needed it. He also kept crates and crates of Coca Cola and other soft or fizzy drinks there. I don't know why he kept the goods there because he never locked the shed that is, until one night …

The shed got raided! It was Guy Fawkes Night and it happened while Jack and his family were out in the park watching the fire works display.

Jack almost caught the raiders red handed when he came back to the house to go to the dunny unexpectedly. He happened to see the garage side door slightly open. The raiders got away with a small box of *Frosty Jack* ice cream "bombs on a stick" and six bottles of Coke. These were thrown, hastily it seemed, into the fence between "us and them", as the raiders made a hasty retreat.

The next morning the six bottles of coke could not be located, I'm told. The box of ice creams had melted and were riddled with ants.

That same day, the shed had a chain, a shiny new padlock installed, and the hole in the fence was sealed with steel mesh. I thought that Jack was a bit rough in pointing the silent finger at us. He never said anything to Dad about it but from then on he always used to stare at me over his glasses with a scowl. His look silently said, "One of these days you are going to get yours son!" Yet even I had no idea who the raiders were. For once I was innocent!

Nike

I came home from a business trip to the United States in 1978. A family friend in Motueka owned and ran a large menswear store and stocked many varieties of sports shoes. His main brands were *Slazenger* and *Adidas*.

I told him that I had met a bloke in Portland, Oregon, who had invented a new style of sports shoe, which was taking America by storm. His business was growing fast and he was about to start exporting to Europe, Australia and New Zealand. I was selling and racing jet boats at the time and had no interest in sneakers. The bloke in Portland asked if I knew anyone in New Zealand who would like to import his shoes.

I offered our friend the chance to be the sole franchise holder for the *Nike* brand name in New Zealand. I happened to be wearing a pair of the shoes at the time, lime green in colour, and the *Nike* tick and the design was certainly "different" to *Slazenger* and *Adidas*! He said the the style and colour looked a bit poncey and the name would never take off in New Zealand.
Don't we let so many chances go by?

Novel Use For Condoms

Condoms hold about six gallons of water if you fill them with a hose and tie the top off. A good trick is to then place them in the middle of the road at night. When a car hits them the result is quite fun. Water for miles and the car will pull up fairly quickly. When the driver gets out of the car to see what he or she has hit, all they see is a big patch of water on the road. It's funny to see them standing in the middle of the road looking around for some sort of explanation.

Aprons Can Be Dangerous

One day my brother Pat, on holidays from the Army, rode his motorbike home. He came roaring up the driveway and around into the back yard a bit too fast and by the time he got to the clothes line it was too late.

He caught his head in the neck loop of an upside down apron which yanked him backward off the bike onto his bum on the lawn. The bike careered on, under the plum tree and into Mum's vegetable garden. I can still see Mum charging around after Pat waving the handle end of a straw broom trying to whack him with it for ploughing up her garden. "Some welcome home," he said later.

Fire!

Dad had a habit of sitting in his favourite chair in the sitting room and reading the paper in the evenings, especially if it was raining and he could not go fishing. This used to bug Sean, Kerry and me as there were many other things we wanted him to do like help re-build bikes or tree huts.

One particular evening he was sitting reading and he fell asleep. He was sitting there, arms still outstretched holding the paper and the only way we could tell that he was asleep was because he was snoring – and boy, could he snore!

We were five, six and seven years old respectively, sitting on the floor at his feet, as we often did, and were not very happy with his inattention. Sean pulled out a box of matches and lit the bottom of the newspaper. After about ten seconds, the paper roared to life and hell did the old man get a fright. He yelped and jumped up out of the chair, hurling the burning newspaper onto the floor and stomping it out with great gusto. We had slunk back a few paces and watched in awe as he stomped out what was left of the charcoal mess on the carpet. I'm sure he was wondering what the hell happened and I bet he was also wondering how he was going to explain this to Mum. Dad thought that his cigarette had caused the fire. We silently agreed!

Dad found a small place rug to cover the singed carpet and winked at us as he put his forefinger over his compressed lips while pointing through the wall to where Mum was cooking tea. He then raced out to the woodshed and came in with kindling and logs to light the open fire. He was obviously trying desperately to disguise the burning smell.

I remember asking Sean later why he pulled such a ripping stunt. He said that he had seen Dennis the Menace pull the same trick on his father in an episode of *The Beano Book*.

Sean said, "It sure got the old man's attention." He was not wrong with that statement!

Cat On A Hot Tin Roof

Someone's cat got shot accidentally with a slug gun. In haste to hide the evidence, it was hurled, like many other things, over the fence where Eric lived next door. The term "over Eric's" was born years before as a place to dump evidence.

Unfortunately, the cat was "hurled" too far and it ended up on Eric's roof. The roof swept up and away to its apex if one looked out our dining room window.

What do we do now? Pull the blinds down! Mum asked us why the blinds were down and promptly pulled them up. She glanced out of the window, paused briefly, staring outside as if in disbelief and then walked to the kitchen.

We all heaved a short-lived sigh of relief but it got the better of her and she came back, looked out the window again, and said, "What's that on Eric's roof?"

A "three boy" chorus responded in harmony, "Tin."

Tex

One night another drunk came home from the pub with Dad. He was introduced as Tex and he had a big white steel guitar. Emblazoned on its face was a cowboy on a horse throwing a lasso. Tex lent me that big white guitar and I learned to play it.

The country and western singer, came back to town a year or so later. He played a concert in the local picture theatre, had a few beers with Dad in the pub and came home pissed with Dad for tea. He asked me to play for him. He then took the guitar and left! He obviously didn't like what he heard!

Then I realised that the drunk with the white guitar that Dad brought home from the pub, was the famous Tex Morton.

Olympic Champions Galore

One day at primary school, we had a visit from Peter Snell, Ron Clarke, Murray Halberg and a couple of other Olympic Games long distance runners. The next day and for about a week afterwards, there were hundreds of Olympic hopefuls running around our streets! The next week, Snell, Clarke and Halberg were running the streets alone.

Dalhof The Swede

I don't know if "Dalhof the Swede" was a local or not. "Local" being someone who had been in the district for most of their life. I don't know where he lived either but he was so far up himself, he had pubic hairs coming out his nostrils.

A local farmer bailed him up one day, shooting rabbits on the farmer's property without permission. The farmer was not happy and told Dalhof of this fact.

In reply, it is rumoured, Dalhof said, "Don't you know who I am? I'm Dalhof the Swede."

The farmer replied, "Swede, turnip or bloody potato, get the hell off my property."

It was a simple little yarn but it has always made me smile.

Blind Faith

During my late teens and early adult life, I often questioned many of the religious teachings from my time at the convent school. I have listened and talked with people who had also attended Catholic schools in the fifties. I now know I am not alone in asking the "difficult to answer" questions of my religion. All the things I had bottled up inside for so many years. Bottled up because I could never find acceptable answers. I never had faith enough to blindly believe. I was human after all.

The fear of hell, the worry of mortal sin, non-attendance at mass and no confession and therefore, no communion for so many years. No one to ask and no one to confide in. Fear of who knows what sort of retribution, or from where.

Some of the teachings had left an almost indelible mark. I could not shake them off and get on with life. I also knew that there were many others out there just like me. They felt the same way as I did. A great weight had been lifted from my shoulders especially now that I had discussed it with others in the same predicament. I had been too sensitive regarding my religion and couldn't find a balance. Hindsight told me that the "message" was perhaps overdone especially to young and open fertile minds.

We were "baptised" and because of that, we would get into heaven. Our Protestant friends were "christened" and yet they would never make it to heaven because they were not Catholics. Any child regardless of religion, who was not baptised, let alone not christened, would never make it to heaven. They would stay in a place called limbo forever and ever. The same went for all the little black babies in Africa, the Solomon Islands and the Amazon jungle. They would never be baptised and so they too would end up in limbo. That was in hindsight, I believe, probably not the correct way to teach the kids at the convent school. I later learned that the same stories and religious beliefs had been taught in Catholic schools world wide, almost word for word. I take my hat off to the Church for organising this and ensuring and sustaining the integrity of the message, but was it the right or wrong way to do so?

Families were asked to give money to the poor via the Church so that they could send missionaries over to Africa and to other third world countries. This would enable all the little black children to be baptised and then they would get to heaven. Therefore, many Catholics gave what spare money they had to get the job done in these far off places. Years later I couldn't help noticing how spectacular the new schools and especially the new Catholic churches were. Yet there were still poverty and unbaptised kids in Africa. Then I read how the Catholic Church was the wealthiest organisation in the world. The accumulation of land, the monetary reserves, the buildings, the art treasures and all the pomp, ceremony and extravagance. It just did not add up.

How many hours of my life had I thought about those things? Why didn't the Catholic Church sell up some of the land; cash in the treasures and fire the proceeds into fixing some of the problems. New churches around the world did not really need extravagant rooflines and imported stained glassed windows. The money saved could have been used to sort out some of the poverty in Africa, the Solomons and the Amazon. Instead, they continued to besiege governments for financial assistance but a bit of both would have been a good idea. Why didn't the Vatican harness all their Swiss Guards and advisers and fire them off to Africa to do something really useful! My remedies were too simplistic and idealistic I guess.

Looking back, at primary school there were times when I wanted to stand up and seriously question some of the divine teachings. But there were no answers anyway. Even theologians couldn't seem to get a handle on it. We just had to believe it and that was that.

Many Protestant kids attended what they called Sunday school. Initially I thought that was some sort of picnic. I later found out that this was their form of weekly religious instruction. We had our religious instruction every day in school and that's why our school day was longer than theirs.

I cannot recall any religious teaching occurring at home. The closest we got was to say a short prayer on our knees before we went to bed. This consisted of praying for the well being of the priests, nuns and our family. We were forbidden to set foot in any of the other denominations' churches. Not even for a wedding. It was a mortal sin to do so. I often wondered why we couldn't. I was 17 years old when I committed that particular mortal sin. I attended a youth dance in an Anglican Church hall and had to get to the hall by going through the church itself.

Aside from the big one, "Original", which everyone got when they were born, (whether you deserved it or not) there were two other types of sin, venial and mortal. Venial was the lesser and you could receive communion after being guilty of venial sin but not if you had committed a deed worthy of mortal sin. You had to go to confession before communion if you had committed mortal sin. Then, and only then, could you receive communion. If you received communion in the state of mortal sin then you were lumbered with another mortal sin! Somewhat like accumulating interest! So you sat in church and when it was time for communion and if you just happened to be in the state of mortal sin, you stayed in your seat. At that point you wondered if everyone was staring at you as if you were a lost cause. The only way out was to hope that the communion getters around you got the impression that you had not fasted for an hour before the mass. This was also a prerequisite to receiving communion.

Mixed marriages whether it was race, colour, Catholic/non-Catholic were an absolute no no, although the "colour" bit was never written or spoken about. None of my brothers or sisters married Catholics. Yet in previous generations a prospective wife or husband had to be converted to Catholicism if a marriage was to proceed. No priest would marry a couple unless this criterion was met. So I married a non-Catholic and if that wasn't the finish, my divorce some years later surely sealed my fate.

There were two Catholic newspapers, the *Tablet* and the *Zealandia*. Mixing sport, politics and religion "just did not happen" but these two newspapers seemed to revel in doing so.

In writing this, I am not in any way renouncing my Catholicism. Far from it. I just wish that our intelligence had been treated with the same respect that we treated our teachers and the hierarchy of the Catholic Church.

It's a sobering thought that everyone has a dark secret. It is interesting to let your mind wander to an afterlife where everyone is wandering around finally catching up with old friends, acquaintances, teachers, famous people they had read about, and others whose secrets are now revealed. The mind boggles! For example, "That was the truth about the assassination of John F Kennedy"; or "That was the person who stole my bike"; or "That was the person who robbed the Bank of England"; or "That teacher wasn't gay after all"; or "Crikey all religions have been worshipping the same God." However let's hope that in the afterlife all these things are forgotten, and let's "just get on with it!"

It is also interesting knowing people who have never had a religious upbringing, who never go to church and have never belonged to a religious organisation in any shape or form. Yet these same people are unassuming, kind, and generous, and seem to live happy lives. And there are plenty of these people in Motueka. I sure hope they get to heaven for they deserve it, but based on the religious teachings of our childhood, they may not have a chance.

And In The End

From my earliest childhood memories, until my parents passed away, these are some of the highlights with a couple of lowlights in between.

In 1982, after Mum passed away and was laid to rest, the "Three Small Suspects" finally "grew up!" A little late, I guess. The pranks came to a halt. Some will never get to print. On rare occasions however, they get a verbal hiding at weddings and funerals.

For many years, I have intended writing these stories and in finally doing so, I do not, and have not intended to offend in any way. I ask that if any reader named in the stories is offended then please accept my apologies or call me to arrange a time and place for a duel with shanghais.

As children, we were the lucky ones, the fortunate ones. We did not live a sheltered life, in fact it was quite the opposite. However, I firmly believe that we were blessed with the best option of any environment in which to grow up. I have no regrets.

My brothers and sisters have all made it to the half-century mark. None of us has fallen foul of the law or become addicted to drugs or alcohol, although perhaps borderline on the latter. We have all been successful in our goals and in our quests to achieve them, whatever they have been.

In the words of a past mentor and great friend, teacher and role model, and an Irishman to boot, it was Jack Magee who hammered me with three quotes:

You always need a plan he said, "If you don't know where you're going, who cares how you travel?"

You cannot motivate anyone. "You can only inspire people to motivate themselves."

The answer to the most complicated problem or inconvenience is always the simplest. "How often do we look for the most complicated answers to complicated problems when in the end the answer is always the simplest?"

I don't know where he pinched these from but I think of them often.

references

bach *Hut, crib or dwelling. Usually very small. Used as a shelter at beaches, rivers, or in the hills for camping purposes etc.*

blamee *generally me as I always got the blame*

bird *A girl. Sometimes called a sheila*

cop *Policeman as opposed to TRAFFIC COP whose job was solely traffic matters. Both these roles are now integrated in NZ and have been for many years.*

dob *Report someone to a higher authority*

dork *Dopey or nerdish. Can also be a penis or dick!*

doublee *The person who sat on the bar of the bike*

couple *Two*

dunny *A toilet. Also known as a loo, long drop, outhouse, shit house.*

guy fawkes *A celebration on the 5th of November each year where fire works displays are held. Normally an effigy of Guy Fawkes is burnt on a bonfire. Commemorates Guy Fawkes' attempt to blow up the English Houses of Parliament.*

juice *Petrol or accelerant*

lummy *Nick name for Pierce Lummis*

mot *Shortened name for the town of MOTUEKA*

motueka *Pronounced "Mot Chew Ay ka" or "Mo Tu Wek a"*

mute mode *One of my Mother's tricks. She would embark on one of these no speak routines when things did not go her way; or when one of us, including Dad, had done something to displease her; or when we proved her wrong on some issue. She was a walking encyclopaedia. Mum was quite funny actually, when she was in mute mode. She would purse her lips and place her forefinger across them and then she would make a sign as if she was slitting her throat when we asked her a question. Mute modes could last from a minute to three or four days, but mostly they were short because mum loved to talk, almost as much as she loved her flowers!*

NZ *New Zealand*

pie cart *Sort of a mobile diner and take away fast food outlet, usually towed by a truck or van.*

pig butchery *One of the local butcher shops in Motueka had one of the towns first neon signs erected on the roof of the shop. The shop was on a corner and the neon sign depicted about twenty pink pigs running around the corner. It was very effective. Such a pity it's now gone, we all loved it.*

pom *Nickname for Englishmen. Also referred to as Pommies or Pommy*

ronk *My sister Veronica's nickname*

stickee *The kid whose bike got a sticker from the local traffic cop after the inspection*

went haywire *When something went radically wrong*

currency

quid *One pound or 20 shillings. The equivalent of 2 dollars*

ten bob note *Ten shillings or one dollar*

half a crown *Two shillings and six pence or twenty-five cents*

florin *Two shillings or 20 cents*

bob *One shilling or 10 cents*

penny *One cent*

hapenny *or halfpenny. Half of one cent*

farthing *Half of a hapenny*

fart *Half of farthing!*

weights & measures conversion (approx)

One metre = *39 inches* = *3 feet 3 inches* = *one yard and 3 inches* = *1000 millimetres*

One yard = *36 inches*

One mile = *1.6 kilometres*

One hundred miles per hour = *150 kilometres per hour*

One foot = *300 millimetres*

One inch = *20 millimetres*

2.2 acres = *1 hectare*

One pound = *one pint (near enough for whitebait!)*

One kilogram = *2.2 pounds*

One hundredweight = *112 pounds*

One gallon = *4.2 litres*

acknowledgements

amanda gould & melanie maher

Very special thanks for the wonderful illustrations and graphics, and your enthusiasm for getting the book completed. I could not have dreamed for anything better.

sue scott

A friend from my early childhood. We kept in touch. Perhaps not as often as we should have. Sue, thanks for reading and editing the draft and for your support not only for this but for many of the things I tried over the years, some of which worked and some of which did not. We laughed and cried together and will always be friends. Interestingly, Sue is the only person I have kept in touch with throughout all the years since we were at primary school. We weren't even at the same school!

sir pat goodman & peter goodman

Without your guidance throughout my youth and working life, I shudder to think what may have been. You bought whitebait from me during my childhood and paid a premium! You employed me when I needed work, and you followed my progress throughout that time. You always have time to meet with me when I "go home" to Motueka. Yet I am only one of the many individuals, families, charities and institutions you have helped and supported over the years. My very sincere thanks.

greg & judy pointing

Our close friends in Sydney, Australia, who are an inspiration to all parents of young families and who have been instrumental in urging me to complete the manuscript.

jim & teresa carman

You came to Mot, in the mid-sixties and befriended my family. Then in later years, you are always there for me in good times and bad. However, these days there are few if any, bad times.

auntie roie thorn & auntie nessie horgan

For being the "Second Mums" to Alex and Jan Horgan's tribe throughout all these years.

uncle allan thorn

You had the patience to teach me how to play golf to a reasonably high standard. With this background, I travelled throughout America, meeting and playing rounds of golf with some of the greatest professional players of the game.

auntie val & uncle oskars pukite

For supporting me through thick and thin over the past thirty years.

dave batty, my great mate

Dave is a photographer and grabbed a plane from Brisbane to Christchurch and Christchurch to Nelson. Then from Mot, he hired a helicopter, and had it land on the very top of Brown Acre. From there, he took hundreds of photos for this and my next book. As he flew back, he directed the pilot up and down the Motueka River, then over the township, clicking merrily with his camera so that I could choose from over 500 photos for the select few to insert in the book

the sisters of st joseph, gabriel & philomena

In spite of all the things I have written, you were kind to us and taught us well, especially the discipline part.

rev. father (now bishop) john cunneen

Another who kept me on the straight and narrow in spite of my pranging his car on numerous occassions.

my brothers, pat, sean & kerry

You know the old saying, "never let the truth get in the way of a good yarn, or two!" "If you don't like it … up yours and go write your own version!" (Or simply deny it!)

my sisters hilary, veronica & francie

You didn't get much of a mention in the book. After reading it however, you have probably heaved great sighs of relief! I love you dearly and know you have always supported me through thick and thin.

author's note

A few weeks before I had finished the final draft of Three Small Suspects I read Frank McCourt's Angela's Ashes. My brother Sean had recommended it and fortunately, there was a copy in our library. After eighty pages, I became depressed. I thought of our young lives and upbringing in a small town in New Zealand. I tried to compare it with Frank McCourt's story. The time between the settings of the two stories was barely a decade. I seriously doubted if life in Ireland in the '50s and '60s could ever have caught up with the wonderful experiences we had as opposed to the McCourts of Ireland. I then vowed that "Three Small Suspects" would stay exactly the way I had written it for what I had penned was exactly the way it was, almost the opposite of Angela's Ashes.

Our roots were in Ireland and I thank God that the Horgans who came to New Zealand in the mid-1800s got the hell out of the country when they did! When I read my own stories, I know that some of the pranks we got up to would have been much the same as the pranks of the youngsters of Ireland. They were imprisoned and sent to the "colonies" for such unbelievably minor offences. Admittedly, in spite of our lineal heritage, the culture and external influences of each country were obviously very different.

My writing will never be to the literary standard of Angela's Ashes but in reading McCourt and writing Three Small Suspects, I am forever grateful to my ancestors for doing whatever it was that they did to be thrown out of Ireland! Had that not happened my brothers and I could well have been in jail or hanged by the time we were teenagers.

In New Zealand if they still had transportation to the "colonies" as punishment for misdemeanors when we were young, I often wonder where on earth the "Three Small Suspects" would have ended up?

photograph album

Dad 1944. Somewhere in Europe.

The Yank Tank. Lucky not to have been shot!

Mum with her glads.

Mum 1961.

Kerry, Hilary, Pat, Nick, Ronk, Sean. Front porch of 29 Poole St 1953.

29 Poole St in 2008. Nothing has changed except the gardens.

Cricket ground in 2008. 29 Poole St back gate can be seen just in from the right. New cricket pavillion on the left.

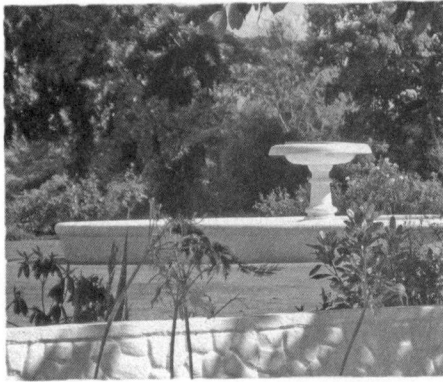

Inglis' fountain … looks different frothing with *Lux Flakes*.

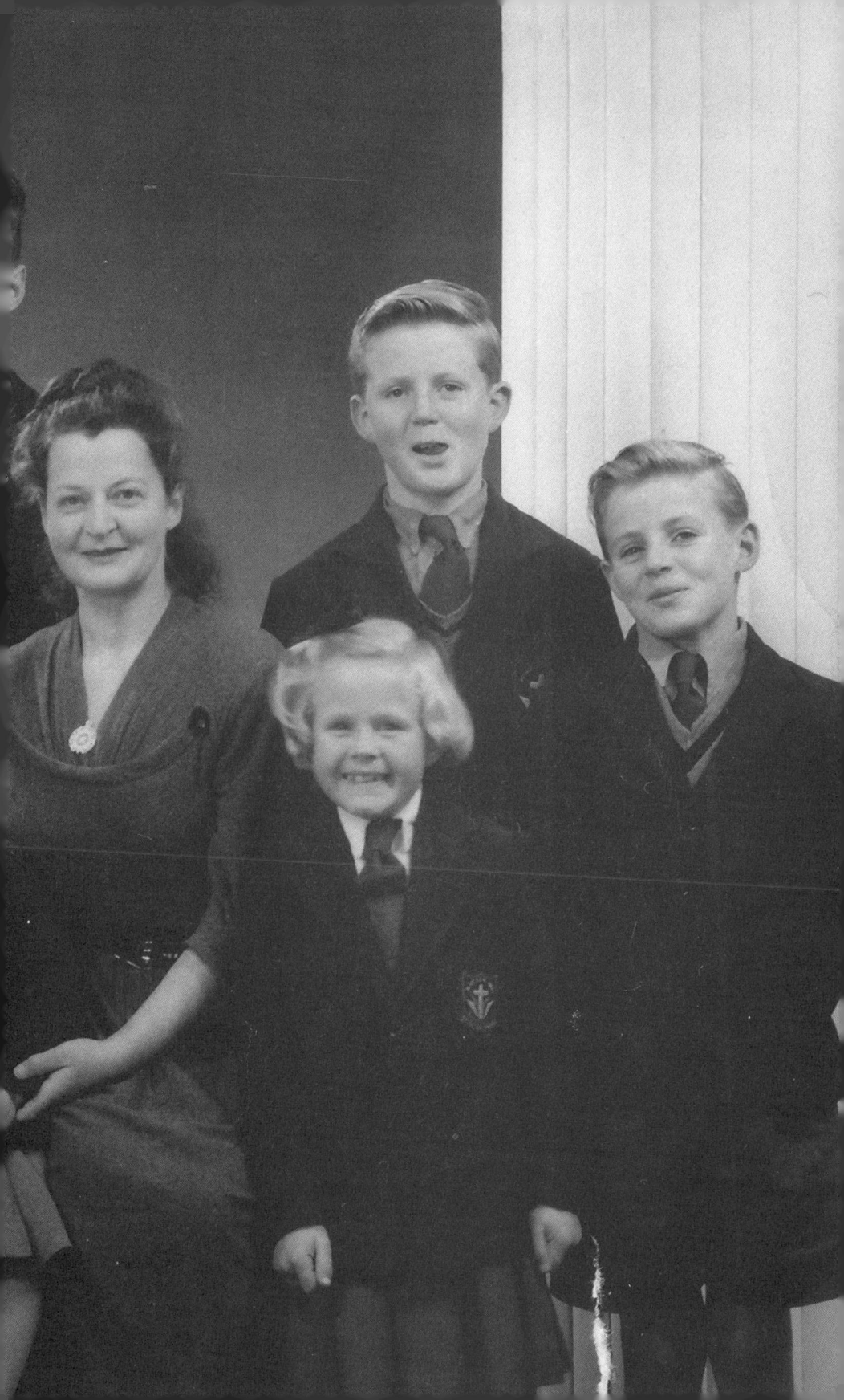

(previous page) Nick, Hilary, Dad, Francie,Pat, Mum, Ronk, Sean,
Kerry. Note the bulge from the catty and stones in my pockets.

Caught in the act! Dad returning from trout fishing at Uncle Allan's one
Sunday morning, c. 1960. He was sprung as Uncle Allan and Aunty Roie
had just returned from the 40 mile round trip to Sunday mass

Kerry, Nick, Sean, Pat. Dressing down. Pat reads the riot act to his younger brothers the night of Kerry's 21st. Pranks must stop. They didn't. Centre background – Lummy.

Black and Ingram's primary school classroom in 1954 and 2008.
Parklands School, Motueka.

St Peter Chanel Convent School in 2008. Identical to what it was in 1957.

Motueka main street in 2008. Tasman and Golden Bay in background.